IN THE EYE OF THE STORM

Stories of Survival and Hope from the Florida Panhandle

Jennifer N. Fenwick

Hope Always!

Jennifer Fenwick

Jennifer N. Fenwick
Visit my website at https://moth-journal.com/
on Facebook @MothJournal
or on Instagram @mothjournal14

Printed in the United States of America

First Printing: January 2019
Amazon Kindle Direct Publishing

ISBN-9781729470480

DEDICATION

*For those who survived the storm and emerged to a world transformed.
For the volunteers, linemen, and relief workers who gave so selflessly as
we moved through those first days and weeks. Your faith, perseverance
in the face of such daunting circumstances, and your relentless
determination to prevail are inspiring and worthy of recognition.*

CONTENTS

In the Eye of the Storm

Say thank you! I want to hear you say it now. Out loud. 'Thank you.' You're saying thank you because your faith is so strong that you don't doubt that whatever the problem, you'll get through it. You're saying thank you because you know that even in the eye of the storm, God has put a rainbow in the clouds. You're saying thank you because you know there's no problem created that can compare to the Creator of all things. Say thank you!

— RALPH WALDO EMERSON

ACKNOWLEDGEMENTS

Hurricane Michael brought so many changes to the Panhandle of Florida. The most obvious changes, to the landscape and the buildings, is unmistakable. Following the storm, the city looked like a warzone.

One thing that has not changed is the resilience and faith of the people in the region. Watching the countless volunteers, the residents reaching out in their own hour of need to help another, witnessing random acts of kindness daily, has been inspiring and life-affirming.

In the Eye of the Storm: Stories of Survival and Hope from the Florida Panhandle is a collection of stories from people who rode out the storm, were first on the scene in the aftermath, who have weathered the weeks since Michael slammed into the area, and who have come from far and wide to assist. They are daily reminders of the strength of the human spirit and the power of hope so needed in the aftermath.

Countless people rode out the category 4 (almost category 5) storm and swear they will never do it again. Volunteers pouring into the state in the days following the destruction repeatedly said they have never seen anything like it. City and county officials promise rebuilding has begun and that the area will be back stronger than ever.

It's the residents though, the ones who woke the following morning to a world inexplicably altered, that are at the heart of this project. The survivors. The broken. The devastated. It's their voices that tell the story best. Their beauty and resilience is inspiring and so worthy of recognition. This is for them.

This book is possible only through the generosity of the individuals willing to share their stories, and their pain and grief with me. They are truly warriors, able to put into words everything we all felt in those first days, and all we continued to feel as our new reality settled upon us.

A special thank you to *Linda Artman*, who in her volunteer efforts throughout the area, came across so many people with broken but hopeful hearts, and stories that inspire and put into perspective the chaos and trauma that followed in Michael's wake.

Thank you to the many contributors who allowed me to use their stories, poetry, and art in this project. They put into words all we were feeling. Their images captured the devastation, but also the hope.

Malinda Adams
Linda Artman
Jessica Ayers and POPSUGAR
Jared Brooks
Heather Clements
Ashley Davis
Jason Davis
Kevin Elliot
Emma Fenwick
John Fenwick
Nichole Fenwick
Erica McNabb Floyd
Jeff Haire
Melinda Hall
Jack Hamm
Jason Hedden
Kim Mixon Hill
Karsun Design Photography
Kristi Kirkland
Sandi Klug-Lard
Laura McManus
Tony Miller AB Nelson
Rebekah Nelson
Johanna Rucker
Lauren Shelton
Cindy K. Sickles
Tony Simmons and The News Herald
Jane Smith

AUTHOR'S NOTE

The stories, poetry, and images contained in this book come from the many residents of the Florida Panhandle who survived Hurricane Michael and who are working tirelessly in the aftermath to rebuild their lives and livelihoods.

Most are ordinary citizens who have risen to extraordinary heights to help others and provide hope to their families, friends, neighbors and towns. I am grateful for their willingness to share their stories and art with me.

The artists and writers who created the Facebook page, *The Art of Michael*, deserve a special thank you. Their poetry, paintings, photography, and reflections inspired and ushered in the healing we so desperately needed in the initial weeks following October 10, 2018. A day none of us will ever forget. They are a bright beacon in the face of such overwhelming devastation.

In the Eye of the Storm: Stories of Survival and Hope from the Florida Panhandle, has been a community endeavor. Each story told in the words of the people who lived it. Many tears were shed in the writing, but healing was also present.

When it seemed as if the world had moved on, we relied more heavily on each other and shared in the ever-present heartbreak of seeing our home laid bare in such an overwhelming way. We became united in the common purpose of moving forward, rebuilding, and growing. Out of the ashes of Michael's destruction came the hope and faith we needed to move on.

With renewed passion and our willingness to do the hard work, we will build something better, stronger, and more beautiful. **#850strong**

Jennifer N. Fenwick

THE EYE OF THE STORM

Raging, violent winds,
blinding, battering rain,
deafening, angry roar,
explosive, destructive carnage,
then silence.

In the eye of the storm.
Bewitching, tantalizing calm,
deceptive, quiet, stillness,
illuminating, glowing light,
for a heartbeat.

The eye of the storm has passed.
Giving way to unspeakable violence,
delivering shattering, brutal wreckage
where moments before was silence.

The eye of the storm has passed.
The winds and rain now quiet,
a world once standing firm,
demolished within the riot.

The eye of the storm has passed.
Annihilation its calling card,
broken, battered landscape,
no corner left unmarred.

The eye of the storm has passed.
With dawn's first gleaming light,
the magnitude of the struggle,
laid bare in clear, plain sight.

The eye of the storm has passed.
The struggle begins anew,
with day's first dawning breath,
lay mountains that must be moved.

The eye of the storm has passed.
Unvanquished we remain,
carrying thoughts of days before,
into a world inexplicably changed.

The eye of the storm has passed.
Through the days and weeks ahead,
the seemingly endless violence,
giving way to hope instead.

The eye of the storm has passed.
Undefeated by its cruelty,
hearts and shoulders squared,
prepared to embrace our duty.

Extraordinary, valiant efforts,
beautiful, selfless sacrifice,
faithful, unrelenting hearts,
strong, indomitable will,
recovering.

Tireless, unceasing strength,
determined, unwavering focus,
abiding, steadfast hope,
abundant, inexhaustible faith,
rebuilding.

—Jennifer N. Fenwick, *November 24, 2018*

THE BIRTH OF A MONSTER

by Jennifer N. Fenwick

In the first week of October 2018, a cluster of thunderstorms was observed off the Yucatan peninsula. On October 6, the system was declared a potential tropical cyclone. On October 7, the strengthening tropical storm was named Michael. On October 8, Hurricane Michael was being tracked and expected to hit the Florida Panhandle by the middle of the week, a category 2 or 3 storm. Michael, however, wasn't finished strengthening, it's barometric pressure continuing its downward trend.

According to *National Geographic*, "Warm waters, low wind shear, and a tight core are the three most essential features hurricanes need to gain strength." Michael took advantage of all three as he moved into the Gulf of Mexico and over the course of the night on October 9, became catastrophically strong.

On October 10, 2018, Hurricane Michael made landfall at approximately 12:15 p.m. along the Florida Panhandle. A deadly category 4 storm with sustained winds of 155-mph, gusts reaching a staggering 185-mph, and a minimum central pressure of 919 millibars, Michael made his presence known as the third strongest hurricane on record to hit the U.S.

In the days prior, residents had prepared, waited, and watched. Evacuation zones had been established by the Emergency Operations Centers (EOCs) of the cities directly in Michael's path. Those within the affected areas had either evacuated or prepared to ride out the storm.

Tuesday night, October 9, residents went to bed to a potential category 2 or 3 storm. Many had remained through Opal (1995) and Ivan (2004) and felt confident they could weather this one as well. Overnight though, the monster grew and by 4:00 a.m., Michael had reached category 4, almost category 5 status.

Within hours the potential category 3 impact had grown into a nightmare of monster proportions. Residents rushed to get to safety or hunkered down where they were, hoping, praying for a miracle.

"I think that if people are comparing storms, what was really fascinating was that Michael was still intensifying when it was making landfall, which is similar to Hurricane Camille also intensifying as it moved inland," said AccuWeather Senior Meteorologist Dan Kottlowski, in an article that appeared in *National Geographic*. "Other storms, like Hurricane Opal in 1995, actually went from a category 4 to 3, just like most storms that make landfall on the Gulf Coast tend to weaken."

According to the *National Geographic* article posted on October 11, Hurricane Michael had one last reconnaissance aircraft mission before landfall. The mission suggested it was strengthening leading up to its Florida strike, with reports that the flight level winds had increased, and pressure had continued to drop even further to 917 millibars.

According to the *Tallahassee Democrat*, "Michael's intensification began on Tuesday, October 9 and continued until the minute it made landfall. In that 36-hour time-frame, Michael's maximum sustained winds increased by 55 knots while central pressure plunged by 54 millibars."

Michael's intensification had catastrophic implications for the Florida Panhandle, as peak winds slammed into the area, meeting or exceeding the 155-mph documented speed.

"Hurricanes intensifying prior to landfall are able to carry destructive winds much farther inland than non-intensifying storms, particularly when coupled with Michael's forward speed exceeding 15-mph," the *Democrat* reported.

Hurricane Michael's intensification from a category 2 to a category 4 hurricane occurred in a matter of hours over the course of Tuesday night, October 9. Residents awoke to a dramatically different scenario than the one they had gone to bed with the evening before. The window of opportunity to evacuate had already closed. People were forced to attempt to reach rapidly filling shelters or to ride out the storm where they were.

In an October 10, teleconference organized by FEMA, Brad Kieserman, vice-president for disaster operations and logistics for the American Red Cross said, "This storm went from a tropical storm to a projected category 3 at landfall in six hours yesterday. It's not behaving normally. It intensified extremely quickly. It didn't give anyone time to do much. And the one thing you can't get back in a disaster is time."

As the sun was beginning to set on the evening of October 10, residents in the path of Hurricane Michael emerged to a nightmare. Franklin County Sheriff, A.J. Smith told the *Washington Post*, "We're kind of getting crushed. It's horrific."

Search and recovery began immediately with teams from around Florida deployed to the Panhandle. In Mexico Beach, where the eye of the storm crossed, rescue teams used dogs to comb through the piles of rubble and mangled structures of the once pristine seaside town. Authorities explained that it could be weeks or months before anything approaching "normal" returned to the region.

In the first few weeks following the storm, residents in the Florida Panhandle struggled to come to grips with the destruction of their homes and cities. "Many who have returned since the storm are living in campers, tents or bunking with neighbors, and relying on portable toilets and boxed ready-to-eat meals provided by FEMA, the Red Cross or other volunteers," reported *The Guardian*.

First responders made their way into Mexico Beach as soon after the storm as they could. Roads had to be cleared of debris. Search and rescue began almost immediately in the devasted coastal community. *Photo by Brandon Perdue/iStock*

Like the acres and acres of felled trees, power poles were snapped by the 155-mph wind, power lines were downed by trees and limbs, and substations were damaged leaving literally hundreds of thousands without power. Linemen from all over the country worked 16-hour days trying to restore power. In all, about 6,000 tree service and line workers were deployed to the area within a matter of hours, *the Pensacola Journal* reported.

As this book is being written, relief efforts are ongoing. The accumulated piles of debris are slowly being removed and discarded. Power restoration has largely been completed. People are returning to their homes, if they are still standing, and their jobs, if they are still employed. School has slowly resumed, with an alternating schedule as students are sharing buildings as damaged campuses are rebuilt and repaired. Residents are getting used to this "new normal" they find themselves traversing, "One day at a time," the mantra reverberated throughout the region.

"It's going to be a long recovery process," Callaway Mayor, Pam Henderson explained in an article published by *Panama City Living Magazine*, "You know, you can't undo all the damage overnight, but we're going to get it cleaned up. It's sad to see that some of the older businesses are destroyed but, you know, we're getting through and it's going to be okay. We're going to rebuild. It's going to be better than it was before. I truly believe that we're going to improve the quality of life for citizens and we're going to get through all of this."

In the days following Hurricane Michael, residents of Bay and surrounding counties relied on the generosity of volunteer organizations to provide necessities like hot food, water, ice, hygiene products, and clean clothes. *Photo by Jeff Haire,* taken in the devastated area of Springfield, FL.

IT'S THE LITTLE THINGS

They sleep in the living room now

Just to be close

It's a little thing

But it helps

They've given away free meals while their kitchen is down

Their employees moved away

But they're still serving

He got an envelope today from an old friend

In his mailbox

The box he duct-taped to a limb in the pile

It's a little thing

But it helps

They sang a song she hadn't heard in years

Nana's hymn

The one they sang when she left

He's seen hundreds of people in the past month

But he remembered her name and her son's

It's a little thing

But it helps

They found the missing tool under the shed

It had fallen between the boards years ago

Papa's name was carved in the grip.

They left their homes to restore ours

She lost her house, but she made them sweet tea

It's a little thing

But it helps

The big things have fallen

The little things have grown

Look closely

It's the little things

It always was.

—Jason Hedden, *November 6, 2018*

THIS. IS. DESTRUCTION.

This is despair. Laid bare and broken.

Pain so tangible it shatters and destroys.

This is defeat. A complete surrendering

to forces too powerful to withstand.

This is life. Stripped to the bone.

Wound gaping and raw. This is weeping.

In body shaking, wracking sobs

that hollow and numb. This is real.

So painfully, achingly real.

This. Is. Destruction.

— Jennifer N. Fenwick, *December 30, 2018*

Jennifer N. Fenwick

Destruction. *Photo by John Fenwick*

THREE DAYS THAT CHANGED EVERYTHING
by Jennifer N. Fenwick

Tuesday, October 9, 2018—On Tuesday morning, October 9, The Weather Channel reported that Hurricane Michael would likely make landfall along the northeast Gulf Coast of Florida. Michael was anticipated to strike as a Category 2 or 3 storm. Although, storm surge, damaging winds, and flooding rain were likely, the majority of my family had decided not to evacuate. None of us were in a flood zone, and we'd ridden out a few hurricanes in the past, including Ivan in 2005.

Mandatory evacuations had already been issued for some areas in Bay and surrounding counties, mostly the beach, areas below sea level, and those who lived in mobile homes. Over the weekend, stores had already begun to run out of supplies and gas had become hard to come by. Roads were heavy with the traffic of people who'd decided in advance to head out of town.

My husband, John, and I, had decided to ride this one out, as had our daughters who lived in the Lynn Haven area of Bay County. In preparation, we'd stocked up on water, batteries, non-perishable foods, candles, and hope. We'd boarded up our windows, tied down the outdoor furniture, placed our plants out of harm's way, and made sure flying debris wouldn't cause additional damage. The only thing we didn't have control over was the multitude of mature and old trees in our area. They had withstood Opal and Ivan, so our hope was that they'd survive Michael as well.

We continued to monitor Michael's trajectory and strength for most of the day. We also made a contingency plan and asked the girls to pack a bag and stand by just in case.

Wednesday, October 10, 2018—Though we'd prepared, on the morning of October 10, at 4:30 a.m., John and I decided staying in our home was no longer an option. Michael was forecasted to hit our area mid-morning a powerful Category 4, potentially Category 5, hurricane. Nowhere in his path would be safe.

We called the girls and told them to grab essentials and within the hour to meet us at the Panama City Surgery Center, where we would ride out the storm with other family members. My brother-in-law, a local physician and part owner of the facility, provided the sanctuary as our Plan B.

John and I grabbed our things and fled the Cove, where our home is located. I left my new Toyota 86 sports car in the carport because the wind and rain had already made the streets too dangerous to drive in a six-speed car that low to the ground. I knew leaving that the likelihood of losing the car was great, but at the moment I didn't care. I wanted my family safe. That's all that mattered.

In the few hours we had prior to Michael making landfall, we helped the other families sheltering with us and prepared to ride out the monster headed our way. I called my extended family in the area, ensuring they were either safe or had fled. At 11:04 we lost power and phone service. The generators kicked on providing light, which in the darkest moments of the storm was a godsend.

By 11:11, Michael was making landfall with sustained winds of 155-mph and gusts reaching 185-mph. The eye of the storm passed a mere 25 miles from Panama City where we were located, battering the building we'd taken shelter in. We could hear transformers exploding all around us. The sound of trees snapping and debris hitting the building was like nothing I'd ever experienced. Frightened and praying, we huddled together in the interior of the building.

For nearly four hours the storm was relentless. The lobby doors had been breached and we could hear ceiling tiles falling and metal roofing being ripped off the mezzanine out front. The walls seemed to be breathing. We could feel the air pressure around us dropping with each successive hour Michael battered our city.

Image taken outside the Panama City Surgery Center where we sheltered as the storm began to make landfall mid-morning, October 10, 2018. *Photo by Jennifer N. Fenwick*

The eyewall skirted our area as it made its way inland over Mexico Beach, Callaway, and Tyndall Air Force Base. In our area, we never got a reprieve from the wind and rain, but we were together and safe. As long as I could see my daughters, hold their hands and shelter in my husband's embrace, I would be ok.

As the winds began to lessen, we began to breathe again. We'd survived the worst, but the aftermath was just beginning.

In a lot of ways, it felt surreal. Growing up in this area, I'd seen many storms hit the Gulf Coast, had even ridden out a few, but never had I experienced anything like this. Still, nothing could prepare any of us for the destruction that awaited outside our safe haven.

Thursday, October 11, 2018—Thursday, October 11, dawned bright and cool after the storm. The sky a brilliant blue canvas against a foreground of utter and complete destruction.

Early that morning, as soon as the curfew was lifted, my husband and brother-in-law departed in John's Jeep to go check on our homes. The girls and I remained in our shelter waiting anxiously for their return.

Aid was already pouring into the area and search and recovery were well underway. Preliminary reports cited the Mexico Beach area as the hardest hit. The expected storm surge, which we in Panama City were grateful to have escaped, had devastated the small gulf front community.

The once picturesque resort town was simply gone. Homes, businesses, miles of pristine coastline destroyed. The wall of water Michael had brought with him swept homes, restaurants, and other local businesses off their foundations and out to sea. They'd simply vanished in the deluge.

We heard similar reports out of the Tyndall Air Force Base and the Callaway areas where the eye of the storm had crossed. In Panama City, I could see the destruction out the window of our safe haven. Juxtapositioned against the beautiful blue sky, the carnage seemed unreal. Trees were blown over at their roots, others snapped into like twigs, all bare of the leaves that had adorned them just the day before. My sight line was extensive as there were no billboards, power poles or trees to block my view.

I could see buildings without roofs. Others with downed limbs and in some cases, entire trees, resting on what remained of their structures. It looked, I imagined, like a bomb had been detonated leaving nothing but destruction in its wake. I prepared myself for John's return and the news he would bring.

Our home in Panama City, FL in September of 2018, a few weeks prior to Hurricane Michael. *Photo by John Fenwick*

The Cove, located on a peninsula-like stretch of land near downtown Panama City, was home to numerous oak and other indigenous trees, some three to four hundred years old. I knew our home stood a good chance of having been crushed under the weight of one of the many large trees on our property. At the moment though, knowing my family was safe, was all that really mattered.

At midday, after hours of anxious waiting, John and my brother-in-law, Keith, returned. I'll never forget the look on their faces. Shocked doesn't even begin to describe the expression that greeted us on their return. Solemn, shaken, quiet, they relayed what they had witnessed.

Downed trees had prevented them from entering The Cove any other way but on foot. They'd set out, hiking into the area, climbing over and through trees, power poles with downed lines everywhere, and piles of debris. The humidity rose as the morning progressed, making for an arduous trek.

Both conveyed that at times they didn't even know where they were. Instead, taking the time to uncover downed street signs in order to get their bearings.

Their first stop, to check on John's brother, Steve, who had ridden out the storm in his home near ours. We feared the worst.

Gratefully, Steve made it through just as we had, although the first words out of his mouth, "If there's ever a next time, I'm outta here, Cat 1, 2, even a tropical storm, I'm never doing this again." We'd hear that a lot over the next days and felt the same ourselves. Once in my lifetime was more than enough.

Steve's truck was buried under piles of limbs and debris, but his house was intact with minor damage. Their mom's house, right next door was also standing. The guys dug their way to the front door to check inside so they could report back to Mom, who was with me at the Surgery Center. A lot of downed trees, damage to her carport, busted glass from a window in her kitchen, and her large storage shed in the back pretty much obliterated. However, she still had a viable roof over her head and a home to return to; so much luckier than many families we would soon discover.

After leaving Mom's, John and the guys split up, so Keith could check his home a block over from ours on the water. John made his way slowly to our street. Watching the video, he captured of his trek into our neighborhood brought me to tears. I didn't know what I was looking at for most of it. Familiar landmarks, gone. If someone asked me, I would have assured them I was looking at a war-ravaged city, the remains stark and grisly. It was heartbreaking.

As John crept up our street, he ran into neighbors wandering the street in shock just as he was. He turned his camera toward our house. I held my breath. I knew we would not escape the carnage, but I was unprepared for the destruction his camera revealed.

Our home a few days following the storm. The once tranquil beauty of The Cove, the miles of gorgeous shade trees and hanging Spanish moss that had attracted us to the area were simply gone. *Photo by John Fenwick*

Chaos. Everywhere. Our neighborhood was hidden under tons of downed trees and debris. Our neighbors walking around in shock, trying, as John was, to make sense out of what they were seeing. Trees once standing proud and straight were now broken and leafless on the ground, on homes and crushing carports and cars. Including mine. My 50th birthday present from John just the year before was buried underneath the large oak tree that once stood sentinel at the edge of our property next to our mailbox.

It had fallen into our newly built carport and come to rest sandwiched between the folds of the metal carport roof that had once provided shelter and protection. My car was buried under the massive oak. John's video revealed the crushed roof, flattened tires and shattered windows of my Toyota 86. The good news? It had likely saved our family room and bay window by taking the brunt of the impact.

The roof over the area was damaged and water had breached the interior room, soaking the wood floor and the music equipment John had not had time to relocate before we raced to shelter.

Other parts of our metal roof were peeled back like the skin of a banana and a hole had been torn into the area over John's office soaking the carpet and destroying the ceiling and insulation above it. Thankfully, the other large tree in our front yard, though leaning dangerously toward the house, had not yet fallen into the room between the two front bedrooms.

Of the once eleven trees on our property, only one remained standing, though it's branches and leaves were gone. It looked desolate standing there, a mere shadow of the beautiful tree it had once been.

John's workshop bore the weight of another large tree across its roof. It would take digging through piles of debris to determine the extent of the damage. Our privacy fence was laying on its side in the alley behind our home.

Thankfully, the main parts of the house were intact and reparable, which was miraculous. Our daughters and their guys had lost their house in Lynn Haven and would need a place to live while the rebuilding process was taking place. At least we could provide them with a safe place to lay their heads. There was little else we could do at the moment.

Rebuilding will be long and arduous for us all. We are reduced to bare essentials, but overall, so much luckier than so many others. The landscape within and surrounding Michael's path will never be the same We have our lives though, and both John's and my families survived. That is the most important thing. The thing we are most grateful for as we stand in the middle of the carnage.

Prior to the storm, our backyard had been an oasis of trees, flowering plants and the beautiful waterfall John had built, all surrounded by the privacy fence we'd installed about a decade before. After Michael, it was unrecognizable. *Photo by John Fenwick*

Having survived our youngest daughter's battle with stage four cancer in 2016, our family was already close. This has brought us that much closer. We are survivors and we know without fail, that God is with us. We have seen and felt his presence countless times since that fateful Wednesday that changed everything.

The outpouring of support and assistance from people near and far is tremendous and heartwarming. Neighbors helping neighbors, strangers reaching across the destruction to comfort and assist. That is the calm in the eye of this storm. The unmistakable and steadfast presence of God is witnessed and felt in each act of kindness, no matter how great or small.

My hometown and this region are resilient. We will make it through the aftermath and with God's guidance and mercy, we will come through stronger and more grateful for the little things. Like the sun rising and setting in splendor each day against the stark landscape that remains. Being able to look up at night to see a blanket of stars and the bright moon clearer now without the city lights obstructing our view. Nothing will be taken for granted. It's the little things that matter most now.

HOW WILL YOU LOVE ME?

Who, then, do I address when I ask the question,
How would you love me in this?"

I have to ask Myself
—not the shaken, traumatized me,
not the disoriented, trembling me,
Not the horrified, terrorized me,
Nor the regressed me who wants to curl back into the
womb,
And certainly not the enraged me
Who wants to strike back in revenge at Michael
Rampage for rampage.

Rather, I must query the wise me,
The me who knows that who I am is
The essence of kind compassion,
Of tender wisdom,
Of the nurturing mother and protecting father.

And so, I ask these inner parents,
Who know me better than I know myself,
How would you love me in this devastation?
And the answers come:

We would hide you in the closet
As the ceiling falls,

And hide your lost lamb with you.
We would whisper in your ear:
Peace be still.

We would give you the Truth—
That you are safe,
And give you prayers to say
And confidence to know
The storm will be over, soon, soon.

And when the winds quiet,
And the deluge softens,
And only a soft rain lullabies
The broken land,
We would lead you out, and show you
That you are still here,
That you are alive in this
Strange landscape.

We are there as you pick your way through
Shattered glass, pink clouds of insulation,
Saturated particle board, and wrinkled library books.

And we put you in high gear:
Pack a suitcase, grab precious pictures,
Toothbrush, file cabinet of papers,
Cell phone and cord.
We give you the presence of mind to
Flee.

In the Eye of the Storm

We are with you as the alert, focused, intent driver,
Who swerves among downed wires,
Tree trunks, and prone electric poles to
escape the ruined streets,
safe and whole
In a drivable car
with its shattered back window.

How would we love you?
We would love you to Dothan, Alabama
And route 84 east to Thomasville Road
Past flattened gas stations,
Where you have to hide behind your car
To squat and pee,
And, with just enough cell phone juice,
You can call your Tallahassee friends to say,
"Give me shelter."
And they do.

We would love you through
Weeks of shock—an efficient trance,
As you rent an apartment, wash your moldy clothes,
Buy furniture, and—blessed gift—
Rely on loving friends for a card table and chairs,
Sheets and towels, a futon, a shower curtain.

We would find family friends from Moultrie, Georgia,
Who grew up with you,
to appear with their pickup truck
And take you back to Eagles Landing,

26

Where every roof has a tarp, and your
Sofa and chair weep, moldy and forsaken.

And we would call forth heroic citizens of
Panama City to appear from amid their own trials
To rescue what can be salvaged,
Haul it down two flights,
And pile it, Beverly Hillbilly style
Into the truck.

Now, two months out from the storm,
We surround you with friends
Who share and support,
Who listen and console,
And with the Writing Your Grief community
And the Art of Michael group,
Who pilgrim with you through
Hurricane aftermath.

And we well up in you,
Taking the form of deep gratitude,
You, who are alive at the winter solstice,
The longest dark, the turn of the sun cycle.
We guide you to your inner garden
To plant seeds of the new year.

— Johanna Rucker, *December 4, 2018*

MOMENTS WE'LL NEVER FORGET

by AB Nelson

Annabeth Nelson, known as AB to family and friends, and Brianna Grandberg, like many, had decided to ride out the storm. Preparations had been completed and they hunkered down with their pets and a prayer. It wouldn't take long for those prayers to turn to screams as Michael made landfall.

The bank building, they and some of their neighbors had taken shelter in was not immune to Michael's fury. As the storm made landfall, the windows shattered causing the glass to explode and the hurricane force winds to whip throughout the building, tossing debris around like corn in a popcorn popper.

"They say there are moments you never forget," AB explained, "I can tell you I will never forget this day, the sounds, the feeling of the walls moving behind my back while sitting in the stairwell, thinking to myself, my last moments are here. Thinking I will never see my family or friends again. Wondering if they were going to be okay."

AB and Brianna tried to keep their animals calm as the wind whipped throughout the building and the stairwell doors, where they had taken shelter, began to blow open. They rushed to tie the dogs' leashes to the doors, so they would stay closed.

"I've honestly never been so scared in my entire life," AB said.

They remained hunkered down in the stairwell for the almost four hours it took for Michael to move through the area. The background soundtrack a series of exploding transformers, shattering glass, flying debris, and the ever-present freight train howl of the roaring wind.

The moment the terror was over they slowly made their way out of their sanctuary to make sure it was safe to move.

"Looking around," AB recounted, "I remember thinking, this can't be real."

The First Federal Bank building located on 23rd Street in Panama City, FL, a blown out shell following Hurricane Michael. *Photo by AB Nelson*

Realizing they were now stuck in the demolished building, AB and Brianna, along with their dogs, slowly began the search for a way out. Under the alarms, they finally heard someone's faint voice yelling, "We have to get you guys out of this building quickly!"

Wading in waist deep water to higher ground with their pets in hand, the pair made it as far as the gas station on nearby 23rd Street when AB saw her dad's truck.

AB's father, a local law enforcement officer and first responder, and her younger sister, Bekah, had left the family's home in the St. Andrew's area of Panama City as soon as the winds had died down enough to drive safely. Their goal, to make sure AB and their youngest sister, Savanna were ok.

Seeing her father, AB used a flashlight to wave him down from the back of the stranger's pickup truck they were being transported in.

"Finally hugging my sister, Bekah's neck and crying because she was alive and well. Seeing my dad ok," I'll never forget that moment AB said.

After loading their animals in her father's truck, AB and Brianna accompanied her father and sister back to her parents' home to make sure her mom and grandmother were still ok. After, they made the treacherous trip into the Cove area of Panama City to check on their baby sister Savanna, and her husband, Harrison.

The townhomes AB and Brianna called home were destroyed by Hurricane Michael, as were most of their belongings. *Photo by AB Nelson*

Brianna and AB a few days after the storm, visiting the building they and their dogs had sheltered in. *Photo by Bekah Nelson*

"The whole way I was thinking in my head, Dear God, I pray she is okay," AB explained, "Please let them be ok."

Arriving on the outskirts of the Cove, they had to park her dad's truck and make their way on foot in the rapidly coming twilight, climbing over trees, downed power lines, and tons of debris.

Street signs that would have marked their passage were nowhere to be seen. It took a while to make their way to the street where Savanna and Harrison, as well as Harrison' parents resided.

"Finally, seeing my sister's face was the best feeling I've ever felt," AB said, "My immediate family was safe."

It would be days before they'd know if their other family and friends in the area were ok.

Days later, after being able to see or hear from her family and friends, knowing they were alive and well, was a feeling AB said she doesn't have the words to describe.

"Brianna and I are so lucky to be alive and even though we lost everything we still have each other. That is all that really matters."

A SISTER'S STORY
by Rebekah Nelson

AB's sister, Rebekah Nelson, known as Bekah to all, recounted her experiences that day in the following social media post she wrote three days after Hurricane Michael roared ashore in the Panhandle. As the Regional Public Relations Director for the Florida Fish and Wildlife Conservation Commission (FWC), Bekah accompanied her Dad, an FWC officer, shortly after Michael had passed through to check on family who had remained in the area. The trip is one she will never forget.

October 10, 2018 – A day that I will never forget. A day that no one in Panama City will ever forget. It's a day that changed our entire lives. It's not just that date that I'll never forget, it's every little moment about that day that will never leave my heart and mind.

Moments that have replayed over and over again for the last four days. Moments like the sound of 150-mph wind whipping outside my house. Or the sound of trees cracking and falling on my roof, not knowing if one would be coming next that would crush our entire home. Or the sight of my Mom lying on the bathroom floor after having a panic attack thinking that any moment could be our last. Or watching my Dad hold the backdoor shut while water poured inside. Those moments were a nightmare.

Living through the storm was the first nightmare, but that wasn't the end of it. The second nightmare, and for me the worst, started in the moments right after the storm. The moments of not knowing if my family was alive.

Moments like the one riding through town with my Dad and seeing the devastation. Seeing my hometown looking like a war zone.

Dodging downed trees, downed power poles, and power lines. The moments of constantly having to find a new route because the ones we went down were impassable. The moments of tears rolling down my face because all I wanted was to hold my sisters and know that they were alright. It's those moments that hurt the worst.

Downed trees and debris made roads impassable as Bekah, AB, and their Dad made their way to their youngest sister, Savanna, and their brother-in-law, Harrison, in the Cove area of Panama City, FL. *Photo by Bekah Nelson*

The moment of climbing eight floors in a bank building with my Dad looking for my older sister. Hearing the buildings alarm drowning out our cries for her. Seeing her vehicle damaged in the parking lot, knowing she didn't drive away, but not knowing where she was. It was the moment of searching tirelessly for her until I finally saw her down the street frantically waving at us from a gas station parking lot standing in waist deep water.

It was the moment of hugging her so tightly, both of us crying and hearing her say, "Bekah I'm so scared." Knowing that Annabeth was okay meant half of my heart could feel some sort of peace.

The next moment was needing to know that Savanna, our baby sister, was okay. The moments of trying to navigate our way to her and being turned around any way we went. It was the moment of finally making it to the Cove but leaving our truck behind because a vehicle couldn't make it any further. The moments of walking with my Dad and AB over huge trees and power lines deeper into the Cove praying my baby sister was unharmed.

The moment my second nightmare finally ended. The moment that we walked inside the McElheney's house and I knew that Savanna was okay. The best moment of the day for me was holding both of my sisters in my arms and finally feeling whole. The moment that my heart felt truly peaceful.

It's the moments of realizing what matters most, family. It's incredible that you can lose everything but knowing that your loved ones are alive is all that really matters.

There are so many moments that I have left out, ones that would turn this short story into a book. Moments that will be with me forever.

I have family who lost everything, but we'll rebuild. Our town will never be the same, but our town is still here. Our houses and vehicles may never be the same, but we're still HERE. We will overcome this.

Praise God for protecting my family during this storm and for the beauty of life. Now it's the moments of moving forward, one day at a time. It's the moments of not having anything, but actually having EVERYTHING. These are the moments I cherish now.

Photo by Nichole Fenwick

Through the damage light exists.

Life awaiting the healing.

Time covering the wounds.

Scars appearing in their place.

Signifying strength. A testimony of survival.

All that's broken becomes the catalyst.

For transformation. For the hard-won knowledge,

that even in the darkness, life prevails.

— Jennifer N. Fenwick, *January 3, 2019*

UPROOTED

Uprooted.

Broken at the bending place.

Fractured limbs.

Shattered pieces.

Only these remain.

Cut down.

No shade.

No shelter.

No before.

Only after.

These words not simply a

narrative for trees.

In the aftermath, they describe us too.

— Jennifer N. Fenwick, *January 20, 2019*

Photo by Jane Smith

BITS AND PIECES

The buzz of chainsaws
Awaken me each morning
No need to set an alarm
Their hum as constant
As the piles of debris
I navigate on my way to work
Thankful I still have a job
The streets look different
Once familiar roads greet me
With four-way stops
Marking intersections
Where traffic lights used to hang
Street signs absent now
Stores and shops boarded up
Closed for now, maybe forever
Work trucks passing in and out
Picking up remnants of yesterday
Carrying away bits and pieces
Of fractured lives, broken trees
The way things used to be
Handmade signs dotting the landscape
Comfort station ahead
Need trees removed? Call now
Help with insurance claims? Call today
Licensed contractor? We can help
And the buzz of chainsaws

Their hum as constant

As the piles of debris

That border this strange, new world.

— Jennifer N. Fenwick, *November 12, 2018*

Piles of debris line the streets at every turn. Remnants of people's lives and homes; broken trees, street signs, and pieces of history that once marked the passage of time for the residents of the Florida Panhandle are no more. *Photo by Emma Fenwick*

FOREVER CHANGED
by Jane Smith

October 10, 2018, the day that changed so many lives. We knew there was a hurricane on its way, but after living here 44 years, I have been through them before, including Hurricane Eloise, who back in 1975, brought 3 feet of water into the house we were living in at the time.

I don't think any of us expected Michael to intensify as quickly as he did. Living one block from a canal that empties into the bay, our main concern was the possibility of flooding caused by storm surge. The night before the storm was to hit, (Tuesday, October 9), my husband, Charles, and I decided to sleep in shifts because we knew we were going to need some rest before the storm.

By Wednesday morning, we knew the storm was most likely going to make landfall as a Category 4 hurricane and finished preparations and securing the house. As the rain and winds increased, we chose to stay in the carport, to watch for storm surge. We had our vehicles backed in and ready to leave if that became necessary.

What began to unfold was something that will haunt me the rest of my life. By the grace of God, our youngest son, Ken, chose not to go out of town with his fiancé, instead saying he needed to make sure we were ok. I know without a doubt, had he not been with us, we would not be here today.

It was incredible how quickly the wind picked up, and the rain began. At some points it reminded me of the blizzards I encountered growing up in the Midwest when visibility vanished in a total whiteout.

As we were standing in the carport, we heard a "swish", followed by a loud thud we could all feel. Ken went out into the yard and came back to report that a tree had just fallen on the house. This was no small tree, but rather a giant that was approximately 130 years old.

After Hurricane Michael passed, Jane Smith, her husband Charles, and their grown son, Ken, were lucky to be alive. The home they had sheltered in destroyed in the storm. The loss was devastating to Jane, as it had once belonged to her brother who had died over thirty years prior. It was the last link she had to the brother she loved and missed so much. And now it was gone. *Photo by Jane Smith*

About this time, trees started falling, snapping like toothpicks in the relentless wind. The wind intensified so much, we took cover behind our SUV, believing at any moment we were going to be blown out of the carport. When the rear end of my husband's pickup rose off the ground about 6-inches, we decided to take cover in the house. We had installed plywood over all the windows and felt confident that would protect us.

I think the best word to describe the next few hours was intense and terrifying. Charles and Ken spent the next 2 1/2 hours, holding the front door shut so it wouldn't blow in. Thank the Lord they are both the size of linebackers, because it took all they had to keep it shut. We felt so helpless watching the roof raise and come back down, and the front wall moving in and out as if breathing as well.

Following the storm, Jane Smith and her family had to vacate their damaged home. The structure couldn't be saved. *Photo by Jane Smith*

Since the back of the house was now missing, we quickly found ourselves standing in about 3 inches of water, the rain too intense to keep out. At this point, we truly believed we were going to die.

"Ken I just want you to know I love you, because we are going to die," my husband said looking at our son from where they were still holding the door.

Being in a house that was boarded up made being able to see what was happening outside very difficult. We huddled. We waited. We prayed.

When things calmed down a bit we finally ventured outside. Nothing, and I stress NOTHING, could have prepared us for what we saw. I think at this point we went into shock. It looked as if a bomb had gone off and the silence was eerie.

All we could see everywhere we looked was downed trees, *all* the trees. Those that did still stand looked like barren twigs. Most every house in view had fallen trees on their roofs, in their yards, on their fences. They were everywhere.

We walked around like zombies. We saw the destruction, but just couldn't comprehend it. Even now, some things remain a blur. I think I intentionally blocked it out as much as I could because of the pain that came with it.

As I write this, the new chapter of our lives has begun, unfortunately not by choice. Our house has been demolished, but we will rebuild. We will be stronger than ever, because you can't go through something this traumatic and not be. God spared us that day, and the fact that nothing can ever be taken for granted, and things can change in the blink of an eye, was definitely reiterated. We are forever changed.

BROKEN SURVIVOR

Part of me doesn't want to go,

but I feel I need to.

I'm almost there,

trying to take deep breaths,

but that isn't working.

I try to swallow, but with the big lump

in my throat, I can't swallow at all.

I thought I was prepared for this, but

who could prepare for anything like this?

Please be gentle with the past 34 years

you are scooping up with your claw.

You are taking my baby albums,

and my wedding album,

that was buried in the rubble.

I see my wedding dress and veil,

hanging from your claw

and blowing in the wind.

Please be gentle with it.

The truck driver waves at me as he goes by.

Please be gentle with your precious cargo,

my life in the back of your truck.

I am a survivor though, not just in this, but also breast

cancer.

I stay in survivor mode.

As for today, just today, this survivor is broken.

— Jane Smith, *November 20, 2018*

One of the hardest days for Jane Smith, was seeing her home being leveled. *Photo by Jane Smith*

WORSHIP WHERE YOU ARE

by Jennifer N. Fenwick

Pastor Ivan Beach reminded Bayside Church members in a message shortly after the storm, "God is still taking care of His people and He will provide and pour out blessings if we are faithful and trust in Him."

Bayside Church, located in the heart of downtown Panama City next to Bay High School, had just signed the sale documents for their church property and purchased a new building a few miles away when Hurricane Michael struck on that fateful Wednesday. The newly remodeled Tommy Oliver Stadium, location for most of the local high school football games and graduations, required additional parking and the City had purchased the church's property to make room for the new lot. Michael destroyed both church structures.

Yet, the first Sunday following the storm, the members met in the parking lot of their devastated church, along with Elevation Life Church members who had also lost their building, to worship with grateful hearts.

"Hurricane Michael may have destroyed our churches," said Bayside member, Jan Soper, "but he couldn't keep us from gathering to worship."

With chairs placed beside the remains of their former building and a large tree that survived the storm as the backdrop, members gathered on the unseasonably cool Sunday morning to sing, pray, and fellowship with thankful hearts.

With voices raised in song, the service could be heard throughout the surrounding neighborhood.

Following the service, members, guests, and residents in the area enjoyed a much-appreciated hot meal of hamburgers and hotdogs. Church members went throughout the neighborhood to invite residents to join in the feast. After lunch, truckloads of collected and donated items like clothing, hygiene items, diapers, wipes, bags of groceries, water and other needed items were delivered throughout the community.

"We may have lost a building. Some of us have lost our homes. Some of us have lost everything," explained member, Ashley Davis, "But today, we were able to love on and encourage one another in person."

The following Sunday brought another parking lot service and some much-needed good news. Mr. Todd Herendeen, a local businessman and entertainer with a large theater facility located on Panama City Beach, offered his building to Bayside and Elevation Life for use while their buildings are being rebuilt and repaired.

WITH YOU IN THE STORM

I am with you in the storm,
In the blinding waves and wind.
Know that I am there,
On Me you can depend.

Standing in the middle,
Of the chaos left behind.
I'm holding back the waters,
You'll withstand the rising tide.

I never promised freedom,
From the toils this life bestows.
I promised I would guide you,
Through the hardest trials and woes.

This life was meant to test you,
So, you'd seek Me through it all.
Knowing that I answer,
Every time you call.

There is no greater solace,
Than the peace you'll find in Me.
Even in the struggle,
I'll fulfil your every need.

My promise is forever,
I'll not forsake you in the storm.
My shield and strength I give you,
Against the darkness that has formed.

Through the darkness I will find you,
And with grace I'll light your way.
Through the valleys deep and daunting,
Into a bright new day.

— Jennifer N. Fenwick, *October 14, 2018*

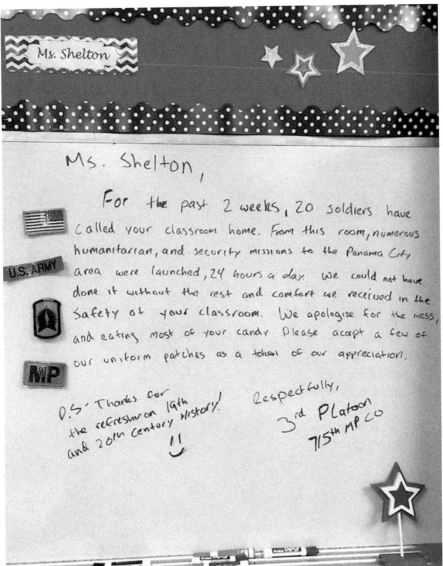

Ms. Shelton,

For the past 2 weeks, 20 soldiers have called your classroom home. From this room, numerous humanitarian, and security missions to the Panama City area were launched, 24 hours a day. We could not have done it without the rest and comfort we received in the safety of your classroom. We apologize for the mess, and eating most of your candy. Please accept a few of our uniform patches as a token of our appreciation.

P.S. Thanks for the refresher on 19th and 20th century history! ☺

Respectfully,
3rd Platoon
715th MP CO

While other schools were destroyed, Lauren Shelton's classroom was made into a home for twenty soldiers. "Although this sweet note left on my board made me ugly cry, I am so grateful to these twenty brave individuals who ate all my classroom candy and helped our town for two long weeks after the storm." —*Lauren Shelton, teacher at Deane Bozeman School.*

THE SECOND FIRST

The first day of school
Comes late this year
Or maybe early
Not sure
We've lost track of time
Students nervous
Teachers too
Most have done this many times
But
Not like this
Not in borrowed rooms
Not in borrowed clothes
Not with so many hungry
To learn
Is the goal
So many distractions
So many unknowns
They need each other
We all do
We always have
WE just forgot
But
We're learning
And that's why we're here
Right?

— Jason Hedden, *November 5, 2018*

Jennifer N. Fenwick

A young boy walks through piles of debris on his first day back to school following the storm. *Photo by Cindy K. Sickles (Cover)*

THROUGH THE MIST

Through the mist, distorted, barren,

this altered landscape emerges.

What eyes drink in breaks the strongest heart.

What feet roam over steals the slightest breath.

These scars, they hurt. Bleeding. Broken. Heavy.

Where does life begin in this ravaged,

Tormented wasteland?

How do we start over with stuttering, shattered hearts?

Is the healing through the mist?

— Jennifer N. Fenwick, *December 31, 2018*

Mist. *Photo by John Fenwick*

LET ME TELL YOU ABOUT MY SCARS

by Jennifer N. Fenwick

Do those scars cover the whole of you, like the stars and the moons on your dress? I thought that would be pretty too, and I ask you right here please to agree with me that a scar is never ugly. That is what the scar makers want us to think. But you and I, we must make an agreement to defy them. We must see all scars as beauty. Okay? This will be our secret. Because take it from me, a scar does not form on the dying. A scar means, I survived." –CHRIS CLEAVE, LITTLE BEE

Emma Fenwick played basketball for three years at Jinks Middle School in Panama City, FL. Those years were some of the best as her mom, dad, and older sister attended her games, both home and away. She was a natural. A true warrior on the court, winning MVP her final year.

Little did she know that her toughest fight was yet to come. Diagnosed with stage 4 Hodgkin's Lymphoma in 2016, at the age of 17, Emma would spend almost the entirety of her junior year of high school At Shand's Children's Hospital in Gainesville, FL.

Emma would weather six rounds of chemo, the first three days administered in hospital, with one clinic administered round seven days later. She would undergo numerous return visits to the hospital where she'd experience extended stays for blood transfusions or to treat one of many treatment induced infections. Yet, like her determination on the court, she was determined to beat cancer as well. With God's help, she did, her warrior heart rising to the test and beating strong.

When she first saw the images of the Jinks MS gym after Hurricane Michael, she was saddened. So many memories in that place. So many lessons learned, and victories won. It was hard to look at and heartbreaking when she did.

Yet, then she was reminded that like her battle to defeat the disease that had weakened her and the scars she now bore, grateful she was alive to wear them, her town, her home, and this broken gymnasium were no different. Though battered and broken, the place it held in her heart would always remain.

Of the storm, Emma remarked, "We have been flattened by a force beyond our control and the landscape around us bears the scars. This storm has altered our lives and our city forever."

Jinks Middle School's gymnasium in Panama City, FL, was destroyed by Hurricane Michael. Area schools suffered extensive damage as a result of the storm forcing Bay District School's to delay reopening classrooms for weeks. *Photo by Rebekah Nelson*

SCARS

He refuses to get his truck fixed

Cause he wants to see the scar

A reminder of how close he came

They say a scar will hurt on resale

But

He has no plans to sell

He's not ashamed of the dents

Not afraid of his scars

Like the one on his chest

Widow maker they called it

Yet somehow, he survived

He rubs his fingers along the raised healing line

He remembers the pain

He also remembers the help

He won't fix those dents

So he won't forget where he was

Or where he is now.

— Jason Hedden, November 19, 2018

A tree bears the marks of the storm, but also signs of new life. *Photo by Jason Hedden*

THE WORLD CAN SEE THE SHAPE OF YOU IN ME

The world can see the shape of you in me—
Anyone who looks into my eyes
can see horror and dismay,
can see an emptiness of grief,
a helpless confusion of loss.

If you look into my heart,
Floating in the storm surge
on its sacred surface,
lie a plethora of unknowns,
mysteries, double edged hurts.

My media posts reveal the rest:
90 percent of your mature trees are down,
gone from my life is the shady Cove.
Floriopolis has lost its roof,
and with it my safe place to create—
stories, poems, skateboard art.

The mall is closed,
The hospital is down from 350 to 70 beds,
Kids are without their homes, their schools.
Giant piles of trees and furniture line the street.

Every friend who lives in Panama City
has lost a roof,
Or 7 trees in their yard are down,
or creeping mold has driven them
from their home.

These facts are written on my psyche,
etched into my confused emotions,
Made vivid by the actions
of this devastated woman,

still in shock, in trance, in trauma.

Panama City, you have marked my spirit—
You are not who you were before the storm.
you've lost your beloved landmarks, your signs,
your shapes and sizes,
churches, go-to eateries,
healing centers, movie theaters,
music venues.
And I have lost mine.

Maybe some will rebuild,
reopen, refurbish, readjust.
And surely many won't.
The same is true of me.

Some trees will sprout new leaves or needles,
And some are cracked, splintered—
their spirits fraught.
Some will be replaced, replanted,
and will bear fruit
eventually.
The same is true of me.
I don't know which is.

When others look at me,
I want them to see you.
Dreary in the storm's aftermath.
People in Panama City
say and say and say,
"We are not ok."

Can you look into my eyes and heart and see
A mirror of my unhappy town?
I too am not ok.

— Johanna Rucker, *December 9, 2018*

My daughters used to refer to this tree as the "Whomping Willow," from one of their favorite Harry Potter movies. Standing tall in front of the First Presbyterian Church building in downtown Panama City, FL, it is now but a shadow of the mighty oak it used to be. *Photo by Jennifer N. Fenwick*

UNABLE TO GO HOME
by Linda Artman

Hurricanes are fickle things. It's hard to guess how strong or weak they will ultimately be when they make landfall. Michael turned out to be catastrophic. It was a devastating hurricane to experience, especially as your first major storm. Yet, Gail and Mike have emerged as survivors, withstanding this trial with fortitude and grace.

Only a few small named storms had headed up to the Florida Panhandle since Mike and Gail had moved to Panama City from Ohio two years before. None had caused much excitement, and only once or twice had they even gathered the outside furniture into the garage. They had not experienced a storm requiring the deep-level preparations that Hurricane Michael was commanding. Not having experienced such a storm, the input from their more experienced neighbors had directed much of their decision-making.

Then came the mandatory evacuation order for their area. That caused a division in the opinions of the neighbors they were relying on to decide what to do. Some were leaving as soon as they could put things in order, making hotel reservations or planning to stay with friends or relatives outside Michael's projected path. Others were planning to stick it out in their homes with stockpiles of water, food, and other supplies. It was hard to decide which camp to follow, but as Michael strengthened to a predicted strong Category 4, they made hotel reservations at a pet-friendly hotel in Birmingham, packed up the car and the dog, and left with Michael on their heels.

Being away from their friends, their home, and all of their worldly possessions was so much harder than they had thought possible.

Before cell towers went down, they watched videos of Michael's arrival that the neighbors who stayed had posted on social media. It was so frightening, and there was no comfort in knowing how bad things were getting. Soon all communication from home was cut off, and they only had the constant, disturbing views from The Weather Channel. Watching didn't help, but it was impossible to stop. The stress and worry were almost too much to bear. They had trouble sleeping and watched TV again.

After Michael moved on into Georgia, still a Category 3 hurricane, Gail and Mike anxiously awaited word that it was safe to go back home. It didn't come. There was no power, no water, and no way to gather information except for the TV.

When neighbors finally got through with a status update, the news was mixed. The great news was that the 80 units of condos, townhomes, and single-family houses that make up their community were intact. The disturbing news was that most of the trees which had shaded their buildings were bent and broken, no longer able to provide that shade and shelter. Worse, many were blocking the roads. Even more problematic was the accessibility of the road into the community. Downed trees and wires made even walking at the entrance impossible. It would be a while before they could go home and see for themselves just how Michael had rearranged their lives.

Mike and Gail decided that Birmingham was just too far from Panama City, and they decided to stay in Daphne, AL, until it was practical to travel the last leg home. They ran into neighbors in the Daphne Publix and discovered that there were four or five couples from home taking shelter in that little town, too. They learned that the Highway Patrol had placed roadblocks on the highways from the north in order to limit traffic and assure everyone's safety. They were *officially* unable to go home.

When they left in haste, they had given no thought at all to when or how they would return. When the roadblocks were lifted, Mike and one of the neighbor men drove to Panama City and back in a day, just to check on things. They came back with first-hand descriptions of the fallen trees and debris that were sobering in their sheer scope and extent. There would be a great deal of work to do.

Day 5 post-Michael found them back home. The power and water were back on and they could begin the process of putting things back together. They still didn't have cable and internet, and their cell phones didn't work at all. Their world was now their small community with the few folks who had stayed or managed to return. Every morning found them working with the neighborhood work crew cutting trees and piling branches on the street for eventual pick up. There seemed to be an endless list of tasks that, little by little, began to bring a bit of order to their new version of home.

There are a fair number of part-time residents in the community, and the workers added caring for *their* units to the long to-do list. They checked on property, emptied smelly refrigerators and freezers, and swept up debris on porches and walkways. Their world was small, but the people they shared it with were big souls who cared and showed it with action. They worked together and accomplished much, proving that even a small a group of people who shared common needs and goals could make a difference.

Within days the roads were open, and Mike and Gail ventured beyond their gate.

"I couldn't believe 23rd Street," Mike said. "It was shocking, and I just didn't expect such total devastation."

It was hard for Mike to process the combination of anxiety before and during the storm and the incredible power the storm had displayed. It was something he'd never experience and didn't want to repeat.

"I felt a huge sense of community," Gail shared when discussing the aftermath of Hurricane Michael. "It was a good feeling after the stress of the storm. It was helpful and soothing, and it was good for both of us to have something to do."

"I'd never seen Mike so stressed," she added.

Determined Floridians now, they will likely help others make pre-hurricane decisions someday. The lessons they learned the hard way during this natural disaster and the advice they are able to share as a result will come from the heart and from hard-won experience.

Someone, someday, hopefully in the far distant future, will be lucky to have their input.

A number of landmarks and historic buildings fell victim to Hurricane Michael, including the building that once housed Panama Grammar School. Panama Grammar opened its doors to students in 1914. When the student population began to decline, the historic building was sold to a local church for offices and Sunday school rooms. *Photo by Jennifer N. Fenwick*

NOW WHAT?
by Linda Artman

The week started out with problems left over from the week before. LaQuandia's bank card was found to have unauthorized activity, and the bank canceled it before things got worse. She was assured that a new card would be delivered on expedited status, so she wouldn't have to be without access to her money for long. She didn't receive it over the weekend. Monday was Columbus Day, and there was no mail. Everything was getting more complicated in a hurry. Hurricane Michael was coming. And he was fast and fierce.

Schools and businesses closed early on Tuesday so that necessary preparations could be made. Every news and weather report stated how important it was to understand the great potential for danger and destruction from the intensifying storm. When Tyndall Air Force Base (AFB), near her house in Callaway, was ordered cleared, LaQuandia knew things were more than serious. They were dire.

Decisions had to be made. LaQuandia has six children, ranging in age from 7-18. Where would they go? How would they travel? What could they take with them? How fast could they make and execute a workable plan? Where could they get money? There was *still* no bank card.

To say it was chaos trying to answer these questions was an understatement. In the nick of time, there was borrowed money and a division of the family. The girls (ages 7, 15, and 16) left with LaQuandia for Memphis and safety. The three boys (ages 11, 12, and 18) stayed behind with a relative.

When LaQuandia called to check on her boys, she was more frightened than she'd ever been before. She could hear the horrible sounds of the building, supposedly protecting her kids, breaking apart. She could hear trees falling and rain. Hard rain. *Inside* what used to be the house. The wind was loud, but not loud enough to cover the screams she heard above the din. The boys told her they were leaving the house to sit out the storm in the car. It was the

She found one with "kid prints" for her little girl. They lost their home and everything in it. *Photo by Linda Artman*

worst experience she could imagine. She was far away and could do *nothing* to help.

There wasn't a word in the English language strong enough to describe the utter helplessness and gut-wrenching fear that she felt. And then they lost power, cell service, and all means of communication. It would be hours before she knew that her family had survived.

Hurricane Michael eventually spent his fury, but the problems he left behind were even more complicated. The closest place LaQuandia could take refuge with her children was in Tallahassee with a friend. She had just been hired to help at one of the Comfort Stations in Panama City. There was nothing for her to do but drive the two hours back and forth. They needed her paycheck and she needed to keep an eye on their house. The neighbors had told her that they saw her house leave the ground, moving off of the foundation. Half of it was gone. What remained was leaning. Looters were trying to take what was salvageable until the neighbors chased them away.

Some nights the drive back to the kids in Tallahassee was just too much and LaQuandia slept in her car. The landlord said they needed to move all of their things out of the house while it was being repaired. It would take 4-6 months. They had nowhere to go. More questions than answers filled her every waking moment.

Should she put the kids in schools in Tallahassee? Her older children would have problems with continuity in their studies. They were A students, with one in the International Baccalaureate Program at Rutherford High School. Should she split up the family and let some, or all, of the kids stay with friends in Panama City so they could continue school there? How could she best help her disabled child?

Where would she live even if the kids had places to go? She'd tried staying in the house, but the mold had made her sick and the landlord said she had to go. There was no resolution to any of these problems when LaQuandia shared her story with me.

Unfortunately, she is not alone in her situation. LaQuandia, like many victims of Hurricane Michael, are struggling to keep their families together. As the weeks progressed and water and power were being restored, many of the comfort stations began to close, leaving many residents, including LaQuandia, without a way to get hot food, showers, and many of the necessities they needed.

Tent cities began popping up throughout the region as more and more people became homeless due to uninhabitable structures and the toxic mold that soon infiltrated their remains.

It will be months before any semblance of normalcy returns for many of Michael's victims and years before the scars left on these communities begin to heal.

Tent cities, like the one pictured above, began to pop up throughout the region as more and more people found themselves homeless. *Photo by Linda Artman*

BEAUTY IN THE BROKEN

There's beauty in the broken.

In the scarred landscape

In the limbs of barren trees

Standing tall and proud

Against the incandescent light

Of each newly dawning day.

In the people.

In their weary eyes.

In the strength of their spirit.

In their undaunted will.

If you look hard enough

You'll see it all around you.

Life, undiminished, undeterred

Awakening and straining to renew.

— Jennifer N. Fenwick, *November 27, 2018*

Piles of debris line the streets near Watson Bayou in Panama City, FL. Photo by Jack Hamm

I THOUGHT I WAS STRONG

I thought I was strong
Until I learned that your family of five now
live in your car
The car with two flats and garbage bag windows

I thought I was strong
Then I heard how you answered the 911 calls for hours
but couldn't send help until the worst of the storm passed

I thought I was strong
Then I heard how she helped you load up to evacuate
only to steal your truck with your life inside
leaving you on the curb

I thought I was strong
Then I learned how you dragged your family room to room
as giants fell on your house
How will you ever feel safe there again?

I thought I was strong
Until I heard that you drove to the home of each of your 1st
Graders the morning after the storm
to make sure they were safe before you checked on your
own

I thought I was strong
I'm not

But
You are
And
Your strength is contagious
And I've caught a touch.

— Jason Hedden, November 15, 2018

Bent not Broken. *Photo by Jason Hedden*

WHAT IT'S LIKE TO LIVE IN A HURRICANE'S DESTRUCTION

After the World Stops Caring
by Jessica Ayers, reprinted with permission from POPSUGAR

If I were to make a guess, I'd say that 90 percent of all Bay County residents did not evacuate for Hurricane Michael. That's close to 170,000 people who endured winds peaking at 155-mph.

Hurricanes are nothing new to the Florida Panhandle. A lot of people around Panama City, where I live, consider hurricane season a fifth season that falls somewhere in between Summer and Fall. When the news stations go haywire, we throw hurricane parties and stock up on booze and snacks. We roll our eyes and snicker because we know that we'll get a few days off from work and have some extra bonding time with our friends. Worst-case scenario, we lose power for a day or two and see a few street signs blown down.

With the exception of Hurricane Opal in 1995, Bay County's track record has been good for so long that I often wondered when our lucky streak would finally end. I never could have imagined that when it did, it would be this detrimental.

Photo by Jessica Ayers

Judging from afar, people will probably question our decision to stay. They might even go as far as to say it's our own fault. But what most people don't realize is that our City Center was not ordered to evacuate. Only the areas in threat of storm surge were — primarily our beach and anyone living in mobile homes. The irony is that most of our beach residents evacuated inland to Panama City, and Panama City was demolished.

Also, keep in mind that Hurricane Michael underwent major changes between 4 p.m. on Tuesday, Oct. 9, and 1 a.m. on Wednesday, Oct 10, and was upgraded from a category 2 to a category 4 storm. By the time it made landfall about 12:30 p.m., it was one notch away from being a category 5. In less than 20 hours, the storm went from cautionary to life altering. It changed so quickly that it was too late for people to get out. The hurricane's force was compared to a massive EF3 tornado (the third most devastating tornado). In terms of pressure, Hurricane Michael is the third most intense hurricane to hit the mainland United States, after Hurricane Camille in 1969 and an unnamed Labor Day hurricane in 1935.

Photo by Jessica Ayers

My neighborhood was hit hard, just as hard as my mother-in-law's, my parents', my best friend's, my third-grade teacher's. There wasn't an area of our city that wasn't heavily impacted. My family (four adults, one 4-year-old child, and two dogs) rode out the storm in my 1,400-square-foot home. It was terrifying, to say the least. Trees crashed around us, the walls shook with fury, and the wind whistled in our ears like a freight train. If we lost our roof, we devised a plan to sit in my car, which was parked under my carport. It wasn't much of a plan, but it was all we had. We got lucky and didn't lose our roof.

I later discovered that my friend, who lives one street over, did. She, her husband, their 5-year-old, and their 18-month-old huddled in their car during the worst part of the storm after their roof had collapsed. Another friend of mine lost her roof along with the safety of her car. She had no choice but to run outside, into flying debris, falling trees, and monstrous winds, to take cover at their neighbors' across the street. My friend Christy and her husband were trapped inside their home for three days after the storm with their 2-month-old and their toddler. By the time they were rescued, they were down to one bottle of water and no ice. The horror stories are endless.

Overnight, our town was transformed into a weather-beaten war zone. The first week of living in post-Michael conditions felt like living in apocalyptic times. I expected zombies to appear at any moment.

We had no running water, meaning we couldn't flush the toilets. We couldn't wash our hands, either; we had to ration the bottled water we had left for other things — like drinking. After the storm, we moved to my parents' house, where there is a pool. We often rinsed our hands in the black, murky, possibly snake-infested pool water, and then we used hand sanitizer to kill the germs.

We obviously had no power, and no power means no air conditioning in 100-degree Florida weather. It also meant no street lights, no home lights, no refrigerators, and no way to charge our cell phones. Not that cell phones were of much use—more than 60 percent of all Bay County residents were left with zero wireless service. We had no way of contacting one another to see who was OK and instead drove around looking for loved ones. But driving around was dangerous, and there was no gas to refill the tank, so we couldn't drive far. If you were lucky enough to have a generator, you didn't have enough gas to run the thing. There was zero access to health care—our hospitals and clinics were demolished, and nurses and doctors were trapped inside their own homes.

But perhaps the scariest part of living in a city that is smashed to hell is the looters. A high percentage of homes were highly exposed to looters because they had no roofs and broken windows. There weren't enough authorities to guard every single street, so individuals had to take matters into their own hands, posting signs like "You Loot, I Shoot" or "Weapon Strong." One woman had her purse stolen right from her hands when looters trespassed into her home. So many cars were smashed by trees that people were forced to walk around instead of drive, adding to their vulnerability.

My husband, my son, and I stuck it out for a week, but we finally decided that we'd had enough. We also needed to get my son to a doctor. The day of the storm, he'd developed a nasty cough that was quickly getting worse. We drove five hours to Jacksonville to get him some medicine and to stay with some friends, hoping to return when things calmed down. Driving out of the wreckage and back into society felt perplexing. One-hundred miles up the road, they had cell service, flushing toilets, functioning restaurants, and gas. In Panama City, we were fighting to survive, while the rest of the world was back to business as usual. We tried to enjoy our time away, but we started to feel like we'd deserted our home. So, on day six, we made our way back.

Upon our return, I'm not sure what I expected to see, but somehow leaving the mess and then returning made the reality of the situation truly sink in. Tears trickled down my face as we drove back onto the once-familiar streets that were now unrecognizable. Massive 100-year-old oak trees that once provided so many homes and parks with natural shade were blown to smithereens, their extensive six-foot-wide roots lifted from the earth, disintegrating entire yards. The 50- to 80-foot pine trees that populated every street and every yard were snapped in half, piled into colossal mounds that were so high, they blocked entire homes. Almost every roof carried a new shade of blue—tarps were their only barrier to block any potential rain.

Photo by Jessica Ayers

It's been 29 days since Hurricane Michael, and our city is still in shambles. We are eternally grateful to all the linemen who came from all over the country. They restored our power in record time, and because of them, we are able to begin to put the pieces back together. As of now, 98 percent of our county has power and water, but the restoration of power doesn't mean our thriving community has been restored. We have some businesses reopening, but the ratio of open to closed is 1:10. A few grocery stores made it through, but the restaurants are few and far between. Our hospitals are only partially opened, and a massive amount of our clinics were wiped out. Countless doctors, lawyers, and teachers are twiddling their thumbs because they have no place to work. For every five people I know, four have lost their homes. They're either staying with family or have relocated to neighboring counties. Many of our schools are still being used as shelters, because there is no place for the homeless to go.

When I use the word "homeless," I'm referring to the people who recently became homeless because of the hurricane.

But I am happy to say that aside from all the destruction, there is a light that shines bright. The old saying applies that when the going gets tough, the tough get going. I've never felt so proud to be a Bay County resident. We have pulled ourselves out of the rubble and, somehow, through all of the mess, managed to hold our heads high. Our community has become a team, and everyone is adopting terms like **#850strong** and **#wewillrebuild**. Because we know that Hurricane Michael is not the end of Bay County, it's a new beginning.

Jessica Ayers is a professional singer/performer/musician, blogger, and stay-at-home mom. She is a regular POPSUGAR contributor.

Sailboats amid debris near Watson Bayou in Panama City, FL. *Photo by Jack Hamm*

HERITAGE

Within days of the storm we heard the rumors
Like so many others
I had to see if they were true
As I made my way
cautiously down your broken path
I wasn't sure I could take more pain

But

The stories were true
There you were
Proud
Almost defiant
Refusing to bow down
Did you even flinch?

At first, I thought your friends were fine too
They were so tall that even on their sides
They reached high above my head
It wasn't until the sawdust settled that we could clearly see
who you lost
With so many fallen friends
you seem even taller now

October was stolen with the wind
How many autumns have you seen?
I'm glad we don't know for sure
We're not ready to count your rings

I see you have your own fence
The only one in town
The squirrels scurry like chameleon ants across your
antique lines
Searching for wisdom

Hey guys! Save some for us

If we look closely
We see you are just touching your neighbor
Holding him up with the lightest touch
We know what that's like
The holding and the being held

I noticed today that you grow toward the city
Reaching with an extra arm of care
Like mom used to do when she made a sudden stop
Still keeping one hand firmly on the wheel

We all stopped that day
To dig out
To call out
To reach out
To count our blessings and our losses
We are reaching still

Like your missing moss
eaten by the winds
we have taken a beating
But don't count us out

Did you really see
the war between the states?
A sentry keeping enemies at bay?
Brother versus Brother
We're glad you're still here to see
Brother helping Brother

We need you Sentry, still
Guard us against
fear
division
indifference
Help us remember the camaraderie

In the Eye of the Storm

we felt in those early days

They call the greens that coat your arms
Resurrection Ferns
They can lose almost everything and still return to life
You're not their host but they lean on you
needing a steady anchor to better see the sun

Like a Phoenix on your sacred perch
We too are coming back to life
Stronger than before
The fuel we needed most was merely dormant waiting
for the right conditions to appear

Our heritage
Our oak
You offer an inheritance of
Lasting love
Steadfast strength
So, we look to you

O mighty oak
Protect us 'neath your bower
Cleanse us in your shade
Thank you for a place to rest
when our work is done

— Jason Hedden, *December 7, 2018*

The Old Century Oak, located in Oaks by the Bay Park overlooking St. Andrew's Bay in Panama City, FL, remained standing, as it has for over 200 years, after the storm. *Photo by Jason Hedden*

REALITY

Reality sometimes stings

and burns. Making it difficult

to breathe. To find a path forward.

Reality sometimes bruises

and scars. Leaving marks that

never fade. Reality often takes

everything you have inside you.

Every hope. Every bit of strength.

Reality in itself is not the monster.

No. The monster already came.

Reality is what it left behind.

But tomorrow? Tomorrow, my child,

is what you make it.

— Jennifer N. Fenwick, *January 1, 2019*

Before and after image of Claire Drive in the Cove area of Panama City, FL. The once luscious landscape with its mature oak trees, hanging moss, and verdant grass, was obliterated in Michael's wake. It will be years before the area looks anything like it did prior to the storm. *Photo by Sharon Owens /Google Images*

IN SHAMBLES
by Kim Mixon Hill

As it turns out, nothing I have ever experienced could have prepared me for Hurricane Michael. For hours, I lay in bed with my dogs and prayed. The winds were so strong I was scared to even look outside – and this comes from someone who loves storms, including the smaller hurricanes of the past. Usually you will find me taking some poorly made videos of bad weather, but this one wasn't your usual storm.

I'm not even sure where to begin when it comes to Hurricane Michael. Everything is still so fresh and raw, and there are so many people who lost everything. All I can do is tell it from my experience, because that's the only way I know how to express it.

I have lived on the Gulf Coast my entire life. Often, people wonder why we live in an area prone to hurricanes. Well, let me tell you a little about the Gulf Coast of Florida.

We have some of the most beautiful beaches in the world. Miles of sugar white sand, emerald colored waters, and a diverse mix of marine life. From dolphins and sharks to manatees and sea turtles – I've seen them all. The skies are sunny and blue, although in a second that can change; the heavens will turn dark and the rain will pour. To me, that's the most beautiful of all.

The Gulf Coast has a mix of people as diverse as its fauna, flora, and marine life. There are people here that have spent their entire lives in one place, there are millions of tourists from all over the world who descend upon the area, and we're home to a variety of celebrities—from Emeril Lagasse to Anne Rice—not to mention those who just enjoy visiting. But we're not Hollywood. We're down home, friendly, and you'll find the best stories from a diner waitress, an oyster shucker, the local artists, the people who work in the hospitality industry, or an 80-year-old women you meet at Piggly Wiggly.

There are smaller stores that have been in business for as long as I can remember, yet you will find state-of-the-art condominiums along the same stretch of beach. You'll see tacky buildings that have garish paint colors and beautiful Art Deco homes and townhouses, all combined into an eclectic mix of color and style.

You'll find some of the best southern cooking from your family, friends, or even your next-door neighbor and can eat fresh seafood that was swimming in the Gulf of Mexico just hours before. And if you like both southern cooking and seafood—I make an awesome shrimp and grits!

Speaking of southern cooking and family, my parents had always evacuated for hurricanes. My mom would gather up her prized possessions (her photo albums) and we'd get in the car and head to Dothan, Alabama. As I became an adult, we never had to evacuate because the storms that did affect us were nothing like this one. Sure, we rode out Hurricane Opal, but that was a category three and didn't hit us head on. Keep in mind that we have never had a storm like this in our area—*ever*.

People often wonder why people stay for a storm, but this one got strong fast and yes, we were prepared—with flashlights, candles, water, dog food, canned food, a battery powered radio, and all the usual things, except for Vienna Sausages, because those are just gross. But no one knew it would turn into the powerhouse that it became.

Storm damaged property along the waterfront was widespread throughout the area. Photo by Karsun Design Photography

Back when the storm was just a small one, we discussed, with our neighbors, how we'd all leave if it got too big, but at the time it was coming in as a category 2. Eventually, we were under an evacuation notice, but for the storm surge only, which never reaches my neighborhood. So again, many people stayed, including us.

By the time it was coming in stronger, it was too late to evacuate. We are surrounded by bridges, which close if the winds get up to a certain speed and that can be as little as 45-50-mph. We could have gone up Highway 231, which was congested with traffic while thousands of others headed out of town, but no one wanted to get caught in a hurricane while on the highway. So along with our dogs, we "hunkered down" as they say, and prepared for the worst.

I could hear large objects hitting the house and heard the trees falling on our neighbors' homes. In fact, I heard when our backyard neighbor's large sycamore tree hit their house. Fortunately, they yelled out a few curse words, not cries for help so we knew they were okay. Not as if we could have ventured out to help them anyway. I used to love listening to the breeze rustling the leaves on that tree. It's been around for decades and now it's gone.

As I lay in bed, I would press my hands against the walls and I swear to you, I could feel them "breathe." It was the most terrified I have ever been. I thank God that I survived.

When the eye crossed over, I knew we had to go through hours more of the same thing. We'd lost power, we'd lost phone service. There was nothing to do but wait, pray, and hope.

After the storm was over, we went outside, and it was wonderful to see our neighbors out, some we had never even met, checking to see if anyone needed help.

Our close neighbors had a tree on their roof, along with their carport upside down on that same roof. The church that has been in our neighborhood for decades, was decimated. That is just some of the immediate damage we saw. Then I saw my own house.

The entire backyard was gone, the roof was severely damaged, we had water leaking into the ceiling, the entire privacy fence damaged or in some cases, missing entirely. The porch posts blew away, the satellite dish tore off part of the roof, and trees we'd had for years were twisted—that is, the ones that remained. All of the storage sheds were gone, with years of memories strewn throughout the yard along with tools, the Christmas tree and decorations, and ironically, a brand-new generator.

After the storm, we sat all night listening to the radio. Hearing about the devastation and some of the stories from people who could call in, or the DJs who had weathered it out at the station. It was hot, it was dark, and it was scary. Just hearing a friendly voice made us feel that we weren't alone in the world.

One bright spot was going outside and seeing the Milky Way from the house; something we can never do because of the light pollution.

The other thing you notice after the power goes out all over town is how quiet it is. I remember in *The Stand* by Stephen King, that after the epidemic had affected most of the population, it was so quiet that Frannie could hear Harold using his manual typewriter from far away—it's almost that quiet—other than a stray vehicle or the sound of a generator.

We've since started picking up the pieces. We are extremely fortunate and although we have damage to our home, we know people who have lost everything.

I've seen the best in people and the worst. I believe these trials don't work that way—either you were a good person to start with or you weren't. A hurricane doesn't make you suddenly become a person who will try to cheat people on a roofing job and a natural disaster doesn't make you suddenly care about your neighbors and how they fared during the storm.

Overall though, I know our area is filled with good people, just like the heroes from all over the country who came to help. Whether they brought supplies, helped connect power lines, or worked clearing debris—it's not just a job, it's being there for those who need it.

The entire landscape has changed—we heard that in some places, 95 percent of the tress are gone. Buildings that have been around for a hundred years are gone. Places we've visited for years are closing because of the damage. You can even get lost in your own neighborhood because *nothing* looks the same.

My beloved Mexico Beach has been leveled, but I can only hope that it comes back even stronger. My hometown of Lynn Haven was one of the worst hit areas, yet I know that we are resilient, and it will grow into what I once knew. Panama City, where I live, is in shambles but again, I know that it will flourish and prosper eventually.

While this section of the Gulf Coast may never be the same, we will persevere and rebuild. We are strong, and we will not allow this storm to define us.

Jennifer N. Fenwick

One of the most photographed sights following the storm was the damaged sailboats along Watson Bayou in Panama City, FL. *Photo by Karsun Design Photography*

ORDINARY

Ordinary people with lives torn and broken
sifting through piles that resemble debris
but are instead, memories, precious pieces of homes,
of lives relentlessly altered.

Ordinary people emerging from darkness
to a world battered and barren, reaching out to aid
neighbors once strangers and strangers now friends
bound by this tragedy of destruction unimagined.

Ordinary people walking unfamiliar roads
littered with carnage, unrecognizable and foreign
mourning for a city, its people, its past,
reshaped and overwhelming

Ordinary people rising from the ashes
seeing past the miles of destruction,
focusing on a future burgeoning with potential
shouldering the amassing burdens of those left with
nothing, easing their daunting loads while their own is still
so heavy.

Ordinary people?
Nothing here is ordinary.
Unimaginable, unfamiliar,
Unthinkable and staggering.

Ordinary was swept away by the violence of the storm.
In its place, extraordinary people
extraordinary determination, and
extraordinary faith were born.

— Jennifer N. Fenwick, *November 23, 2018*

Linemen worked 16-hour days trying to restore power. In all, about 6,000 tree service and line workers were deployed to the area within a matter of hours *Photo by Jennifer N. Fenwick*

OUR OWN BRIDGE TO TERABITHIA

by Malinda Adams

Sometime in the middle of the night we woke up and realized we were looking at a Category 4 Hurricane. I'm not certain what time it was, but I was trusting that God would keep us safe and provide a way of escape if needed.

At 9:30 p.m. the night before, our friend, Malissa, and her daughter, Brooklyn, had come to weather out the storm in our brick, Lynn Haven, home. She was a single mom and her house just wasn't as strongly built. She worried it wouldn't hold. So, we made room for them both and went to bed after discussing that it was still a possibility we'd have to evacuate.

The next morning, we followed social media and kept track of the storm via the internet; watching the hurricane grow in intensity. By 8:30 a.m. we were seriously talking about bugging out, but we were unsure of where to go.

Minutes later, I spotted a post by my friend Lisa, inviting those who didn't have a place to go, to shelter at her farm in Youngstown. I quickly discussed it with everyone and responded, letting her know that we might take her up on the offer. It was shortly after 9:00 a.m. when she messaged me, telling me Hathaway bridge had just been shut down and if we didn't leave soon, we would be stuck in Lynn Haven. Within minutes, three teens, our son and daughter, Brendan and Aliya, and the three adults were packed into the car and leaving Lynn Haven across Bailey Bridge to get somewhere we felt would be safer to ride out the massive Hurricane.

Lisa, and her husband Chuck, had built their beautiful home in 2006, and Chuck had been quite the over achiever when installing the roof on his house. He made certain it could withstand 150-mile winds. We put a lot of faith in his construction skills.

We parked our cars in a small clearing where there were few trees and got inside as wind speeds were picking up. It was 9:40 a.m. By 12:30 p.m., we lost power. The storm had, of course, intensified quickly and we sat in awe as the wind and rain started pummeling the house. The comic relief was Lisa and Chuck's Maine coon cat, Thursday, who didn't have enough sense to be scared, or remotely concerned about the debris hitting the windows, or the chaos that was happening outside. That silly cat, just sat there at the windows as they vibrated, completely fascinated with the outside world, his head cocked to one side, then the other, and finding the occasional bug to pounce on and conquer. We kept trying to get that dang cat away from the window, fearing the next piece of debris would break the glass, but he kept going back. Over and over, he kept going back.

At the midway point, the porch fans were hanging by a single wire, all but one or two blades left, ripped off by the winds. We feared the way they were swinging that soon they would reach the window and break the glass, so Chuck, with Lisa nearly yelling at him, ran out with some type of wire cutters and braved the storm to cut the fan free.

It wasn't long after that, that the peak winds hit. That's when we moved to the back of the house, our safe room area, to watch the hurricane from the doorway through the front house windows. My husband Geoff, picked the perfect time to start recording just moments before the massive oak tree toppled onto the house. It took out a corner of the porch but otherwise the house was intact. You can hear me faintly cuss by accident in the video then reprimand myself as I say, "Cuss jar".

It was an awe filled moment witnessing the ferocity of the storm. But that tree coming down on the house was the only significant damage the house sustained. When it was all said and done, some siding, part of the porch and 90 percent of the trees on the property were down and that was the extent of the damage. Our cars were untouched!

The only problem was the road off of Chuck and Lisa's property and onto a main road was completely impassable.

There were no less than 20 trees blocking us from the first road and we were surrounded on all sides by forest and downed trees. We knew it was going to take us days to get out! It was almost impossible to get past the trees at all! So, what we thought was only going to be a few hour stay turned into overnight, knowing the next day was going to be a tough one filled with lots of work.

Two a.m. came, and Geoff and I were awoken by Lisa urgently telling us there was a fire. Their livestock dog had apparently been barking outside for quite some time and had awoken her and she went to investigate. You could see the fire from the house. It looked like a sunset at first, until the sleep from your eyes cleared, and you could make out the flickering flames that were growing bigger.

We quickly woke everyone up, my 17-year-old son included, who had passed out in the recliner. That kid could sleep through anything and had slept through most of the hurricane in that same chair. But as soon as he heard the word "Fire", he got up and threw his shoes on to help. Charlie, also 17, was already getting dressed and Chuck, Geoff, Brendan, and Charlie, went out into the night with a few shovels to put out this potential forest fire.

The ladies sat watching from the safety of the house and speculated how we would escape if the guys couldn't get things under control. Lisa let us know there was no way off the property and we'd just have to pray the guys got it contained and it didn't come near the house. I had to chuckle at the irony of possibly dying by forest fire after surviving a catastrophic hurricane. We knew there was no way that emergency services could get out to us. We didn't even have phone service. So, pray, is exactly what we did.

Not far off their property was a RV that had been parked illegally for who knows how long. Lisa, for months had been calling code enforcement and reporting it to police to try and get someone to do something about it. She knew it was an operational meth lab, but no one would do anything about it. This RV was in the middle of the woods and sometime after the hurricane, in the middle of the night, something caught fire and set the entire thing ablaze!

For two hours we sat up, waiting on the guys to come back. We saw the flames start to dim and then soon we couldn't see much of a glow at all. In the meantime, unbeknownst to us, the guys had managed to contain it, my husband had taken videos of it, and they decided to go on a hike, through the tangle of trees out to the road to see the amount of devastation. They didn't come back until around 4:30 a.m. I don't know about Lisa, but I was getting worried, not knowing what was going on and if they were safe. Without phones or text messaging available, we were literally in the dark. It's amazing how reliant we become on that instant information and how quickly communication becomes important.

It was during our wait that Malissa and I discussed our tentative plan to hike out the next morning to check on the houses.

We all got a few hours' sleep when the guys came back, and then they got started with chain saws and axes attacking the downed trees, so we could reach the outside world. Malissa and I packed backpacks, water, first aid supplies, and by 11 a.m., set out to hike back into Panama City.

I gave my husband a kiss and promised that if by 3:00 p.m. we weren't more than halfway we would turn back and come home.

Commissioned Painting of Shell Island by Malinda Adams completed just three days prior to Hurricane Michael.

Malissa and I trekked through mud, climbed trees, forced our way through tangled vines, and navigated downed power lines to get out to the road. It was probably a good half mile of navigating downed trees all along the private road leading up to Chuck and Lisa's property.

Once we got to the main road, we saw evidence of people already clearing roads and chainsaws were heard in the distance. We passed people trying to clean up as we hiked our way to HWY 388. We hadn't gone far on 388 when a friendly couple stopped and asked us if we needed a ride. They thankfully, took us up HWY 231 into the Bayou George area and dropped us off at the end of Malissa's impassible road. We were able to hike, climb over a few more trees, and under a few more downed power lines to get to her house, the entire time praying her house was intact and her animals OK.

As we reached her driveway, we picked up the pace, her hands were shaking as she grabbed her keys in anticipation. When we reached her porch, we were both crying, laughing, and so thankful the house was still standing. When she got inside, we cried harder, seeing that the dogs and cats were OK!

There were holes in the roof, the siding was gone in parts, things were wet of course, but it was still there. The trampoline had somehow flown over the house and was in the woods behind it. Her second vehicle, her minivan, was untouched and so was her shed.

Her yard was a swamp, with water more than ankle deep, but we slugged through the water and started digging out the unused generator she'd bought on clearance 12 years prior after a different hurricane had come through our area.

Loaded up with the generator, camping gear, and whatever else we thought would be useful in the moment, we made our way down her road out to 231. On the way we saw the train on its side, the sheds and trailers that had been blown over across 231 and lodged into the trees, and all the downed power poles. We weaved in and out of areas barely passable. We tried going down 390, but quickly realized it wasn't possible and had to turn around. We then made our way further south to Transmitter Road.

Malissa nearly cried when she saw her workplace and wondered if she would even have a job in the coming weeks.

As we were picking our way through, driving around obstacles, I saw someone I knew on a bike. I made Malissa stop to say hello to Bruno. I had sold he and his wife a painting of Shell Island that they had commissioned from me literally three days prior to the hurricane, for their anniversary. Bruno and his family were OK, and he assured me their house had minor damage compared to some. My painting was OK too. I had to chuckle at myself for even caring about something so silly, but I wanted something that I'd created, the memory of what I was sure no longer was, to have survived. Shell Island probably doesn't look the same as how I painted it. As an artist, I wanted to know my work survived.

We continued on our way, picking through streets that looked passable until we came to mine. It was mostly cleared. It was strange being able to see the water and inlets where trees had obscured the view prior.

We pulled up to the house and I saw our giant oak resting on the roof. From what I could tell I still had an intact house but wondered at the orange X painted on the front next to my door. I checked the house quickly going from room to room and like before, Malissa and I hugged and cried as I saw the house was OK. There was water damage of course. Part of the metal roofing had blown off over the dining room, but it seemed like there were no holes. It wouldn't be until the next day that part of the ceiling would collapse where the oak had gone through. But upon first inspection, it seemed like all was OK.

We made plans to move Malissa and Brook into our home.

Going into the back, we saw the giant pine was resting on the back of the house and my sunroom was flooded, after the windows had blown out and the roofing shingles blew off. Just like at our friend's house, the ceiling fan had been blown about by fierce winds and was now just hanging, nothing but limp, soggy fan blades.

The pergola was gone, and my pond was filled with so much debris that my fish were gasping for air. Our shed had already been broken into. I'm assuming someone was looking for supplies they could use and tools. Overall, we were fortunate that we could still live in our home. We unpacked as much as we could from Malissa's car, locked up the house and made our way back to the rest of our eager families to give them the news. We had been gone less than 5 hours by the time we got back.

By the next day, the guys had cleared a tunnel through the downed trees out to the road. Some were resting on power lines or being held up by other downed trees. It was our very own *Bridge to Terabithia*, leading us out to a world that was ravaged by a hurricane rather than

102

a fantastical place of imagination and dreams. We'd made it though, two families; surviving the storm and setting out to begin the next chapter in the adventure of moving forward after Hurricane Michael.

Malinda Adams is an artist and owner of Malinda Ann Studios, LLC.

EXPOSED

Exposed. Revealed for all to see.

No windows. No doors.

Insides spilled.

Laid bare to the stark light of day.

All that was, swept away.

All that remains, damaged.

Unguarded. Raw.

Some wounds don't heal.

Some scars never fade.

— Jennifer N. Fenwick, *December 31, 2018*

Mexico Beach, referred to as Ground Zero. Michael's eye passed over the area leaving utter devastation in his wake. *Photo by Tony Miller*

SIGNS

The signs along the road show the progress of the recovery,
if you pay attention to the messages they send.

Open

Open-Cash Only

Open-Cash and CC

ATM Open

Tree Removal

Dumpsters-Hauling

Need Tarps?

Got Mold?

We Have Bleach

Hiring

Immediate Employment Opportunities

Roofing

Electrical

Plumbing

Dry-wall

Siding

Fences

Demolition

Stump Removal

Public Adjusters

Insurance Claims Specialists

Claims Help Desk

Stuck with Destroyed House?

We Buy Houses in any Condition

Legal Help With Claims

The first signs were serving such basic needs.

As the progress was inching along,

the signs addressed the new stages.

Now the insurance issues and frustration are targeted.

The enormity of it all.

— Linda Artman, *December 5, 2018*

Signs. *Photo by Linda Artman*

DAVID, MICHAEL, & IRENE

by Kevin Elliot

David watched the cyclone approach on the Weather Channel.

"Gonna be bad," he said.

Irene looked out the window at the bayou.

"Worse than Opal?" she asked.

"Afraid so." Hurricane Opal had hit hard in 1995, mostly storm surge that covered David and Irene's waterfront yard in two feet of saw grass and muck. Took a month to haul it all away. The azaleas never came back.

"Is it too late to leave?" said Irene.

"We'd get stuck in traffic at this point," David said. "I don't want to leave anyway."

David and Irene had lived in their home nearly four decades. They never had kids, so they built the place just for them. The core of the house was on stilts, with living space up top, carport and storage underneath. What made the structure special, though, was the exterior.

Before retirement, David was an industrial engineer for a paper company, so he and Irene had travelled around the world from paper mill to paper mill as needed. Their favorite was in Japan. They spent three years on the island early in David's career and the couple never lost their love of the aesthetic. David was able to retire early and,

108

when he and Irene settled on the woody lot on Cook's Bayou, they decided to build a little piece of Japan to live in.

The house was sided and skirted with cedar clapboards almost to the ground, giving the place instant age. The framing underneath was flared at the bottom to mimic the upturned corners of a classic Japanese temple. The side of the house facing the bayou was largely glass. From the living room looking out, it felt like standing at the prow of a massive junk making harbor.

When the house was built, David insisted that none of the towering live oaks be removed. The back deck (again, on the second level) was built around one muscular specimen. The tree looked like a giant's arm had burst through the planks and was grabbing the house.

The whole place resembled a mythic Asian treehouse, suspended mid-air by old magic.

"The storm didn't look that serious yesterday," Irene said.

"It wasn't," David said. "It was a two yesterday. Four now, and growing."

Hurricanes are rated in strength from one to five. Most Floridians won't get out of bed for anything less than a three. Even then, the cyclones tend to weaken quickly as they approach the northern Gulf Coast.

"What should we do?" asked Irene.

David pondered the news cast a moment longer. "Nothing much to do. Just ride it out."

The morning sky had already darkened. Wind was up. The bayou was getting angry.

"Gonna be bad," David mumbled again.

It was 7:30. Time for breakfast. David looked at the oversized digital clock from his worn chair in front of the TV, wondering if it was worth the effort of getting up. Moving about was such an ordeal these days. David was 89-years-old and had refused to get the hip and knee replacements for which his doctors and friends advocated. Both legs were effectively locked, operating like two fence posts strapped to David's waist. His only movement was accomplished by toddling over a walker, body bent at 45-degrees. At this point, his balance was shot as well. He had fallen off the stairs into his sunken living room three times. Well, three times that injured him so badly he had to call friends for help. He was embarrassed to tell how many more there were besides.

It wasn't always like this, of course. Twenty years ago, he and Irene were renowned for their vigorous morning walks down Poston Road, the dirt lane connecting their little community of neighbors with State Highway 2297 and the rest of Panama City. David would march along quicker than Irene, swinging his cedar walking staff in time. He would periodically turn back and do a wide circle around Irene, so he could keep his pace but never got too far from her.

Had to quit their walks as Irene's sight faded. She protested that she was fine to continue, but David new better and didn't want her to fall. She eventually went blind.

"Time to eat, sweetheart," Irene said, knowing David's thoughts.

"Nah, I'm fine. Not real hungry. I'll eat an early lunch." David reached for the newspaper on the TV tray by his chair.

"No sir. Now. You know the power will go out soon and you won't be able to open the fridge for a while. Up."

David surrendered, took a deep breath, and started the process of getting upright.

Fifteen minutes later, he opened the fridge and considered the options.

"Joel brought that pot roast last night, have some of that warmed over," Irene instructed from the living room.

"Okay."

As David's arthritic fingers grappled with the Tupperware, he stared out the kitchen window over Cook's Bayou. A pelican hovered

10-meters up, beak to the building storm, as if testing the wind speed with his floppy pouch.

Cooks Bayou before Hurricane Michael. *Photo by Kevin Elliot*

David and Irene loved this view the moment they saw it 40 years ago. Cook's Bayou is a tiny shallow offshoot of East Bay, a massive descending arm of the St. Andrew Bay water system at the heart of the Florida Panhandle. From his kitchen window, David could see the bayou in all directions—to the north, Oliver Creek, the headwater of the bayou, and to the southwest, the open water where Cook meets East Bay on its way to the Gulf of Mexico.

Cook Bayou's shore was not white like Panama City Beach, but a light tan from years of soaking in brackish water. A prickled thicket of saw grass lined the bank in most places, rimming the shoreline like a hedgerow. Pines, oaks, and redcedars grew to the waterline, twining into a mottled canopy over the house and out over the water as if trying to shade the blue crabs scuttling underneath. Mullet, trout, and redfish were plentiful, which attracted schools of porpoise, playfully spouting and mercilessly feeding in turn.

David and Irene instantly knew they would spend the rest of their lives here.

The pelican wheeled and flew for shelter. And David knew, it was today. He put the roast back in the fridge and labored to his bedroom.

David sat on the edge of his bed and slowly looked around. How many nights had they spent in this room? His engineer's mind had to calculate the number. Thirty-seven years times 365–minus our travel times–somewhere around 13,000.

Cruising had been their thing in retirement. On the wall by the closet was a framed paper world map, a red pin stuck on every spot they had been. There were dozens spread over five continents. David's eyes wandered to his nightstand, where he kept his favorite picture of the two of them, from that cruise to Norway. 1978? '79?

He looked at the physical therapy equipment in the corner. A yoga mat, a couple of those stretchy bands, a few free weights. Fifteen pounds should do it.

It would not be cold outside, but the wind was really blowing now and might be a little chill, so David put on his zip-up exercise jacket with the hood. Shoes? Nothing lace up, too much trouble. But not house slippers either. Might trip on the stairs. He found an old pair of loafers he used to wear to church and slid into them.

His walker had a little basket attached to the front. David hefted the weight into it and scuffled out.

When he reached the living room, Irene gave him a once over and blanched.

"No. No sir," she protested, instantly hugging herself and shaking her head. "We talked about this. You promised."

"Irene–"

"No sir!" She cut him off. The color was back in her cheeks. "You cannot do this. It's not right, David. I can't watch you do this." She started crying.

"I'm tired Irene," David said.

"You've been tired before and come back," Irene pleaded. "Just have the doctor adjust your medications again. Do your exercises. I'll be here with you."

David continued looking at Irene, but said nothing.

Irene tried again. "What about Joel? And David and Vickie? They love you and take care of you–it will crush them."

David's neighbors had looked after him when his health started failing, especially Joel. She was 92 but healthy as a horse. She and a few other friends took him to appointments, brought him dinner, called in to talk.

"I don't want to hurt them," said David. "But I hate that they have to help me so much. It's humiliating. They have lives of their own."

"But they don't mind, they really don't!" Irene was desperate. "And it's good for them too, gives them a purpose–"

"I can't Irene."

"Yes, you can!" Irene was pleading. "You're strong, you can, you –you have your life–"

"I wet myself yesterday!" David yelled. Irene quit talking, stunned. In all his life, David had never yelled at Irene. "Couldn't make it to the bathroom in time." Now David was crying. "Irene, I wet myself. And you know what's next. Can I ask Joel to do that? Would you want to see me like that? That is not a life."

The two stood in silence for several moments, Irene sniffling. After a while, she simply nodded her head.

"Irene, you died almost ten years ago," David's voice broke. "I've been talking to you all that time, but it's not the same. I'm still alone. I want to see you again. *You.* I miss you so, so much."

Irene looked at David for a long time, her blue eyes seeing.

"You're sure?" she said, a last frail attempt.

"I'll see you soon," David said. "You go now."

"Okay, sweetheart. I'll be waiting."

David closed his eyes and took a slow breath. When he opened his eyes, Irene was gone.

Hurricane Michael ravaged the Cook Bayou community, destroying David and Irene's enchanted pagoda and forever maiming their beloved landscape. Two days after the storm, David's body was found at the bottom of the bayou, a 15 lb. weight tied around his neck. He was the last one to see his home the way it was supposed to be, just as he and Irene wanted it.

RECONCILED WITH DEATH

by Laura McManus, LCSW

Death comes and goes quickly. Death comes and lingers long. Some prefer the former. Some prefer the latter. We all will die, but the question remains—will we all make peace with death?

Hurricane Michael came and went quickly, in broad daylight. Almost category 5 on the scale of severity, it bore no similarity to any storm since 1969; or perhaps 1992, when Andrew ravaged South Florida. The Florida Panhandle, as far as Gulf County, was marred by the destruction. Beyond Gulf County lies the geographical territories I serve as a Hospice Social Worker.

Some evacuated early. Some stayed behind. Of those, some were removed to shelters or taken via Life Flight to hospitals near and far. All of our facility residents were transferred out of town except for the veterans living at *Clifford Sims VA Nursing Center*, located in Springfield, FL.

When we gathered back together as a collective group of employees following the storm, we began collaborating with our sister offices in the nearby counties. At the time, we discovered that our census was cut in half. We consoled each other, benefitting greatly from the support and supplies provided by our other offices in the Panhandle that were fortunate to have escaped Michael's fury. Much needed fuel and cell phones were provided, when available.

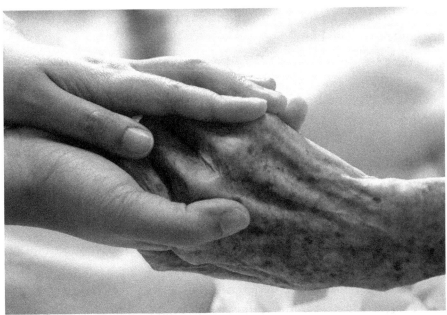

The first routine visits I was able to perform following the storm were driven with great care. My eyes would not stay fixed on the roads, since my vision and senses were having difficulty adjusting to the extreme fall out. *Nothing* resembled the paths travelled prior to Hurricane Michael.

Arriving at each home, I was filled with relief. I was greeted with many hugs. My vehicle was filled with supplies for everyone I was able to visit. The faces and the warm reception was the same, but the homes and the landscape were markedly different. These would likely never be the same. The goal to live and to die at home with hospice, however, had not changed.

Our company has standard emergency operating procedures for maintaining services following a disaster. The *Emergency Preparedness Requirements for Medicare and Medicaid Participating Providers and Suppliers,* that went into effect in 2016, provides the standards that ensure health care providers, like Hospice, are able to meet the needs of their patients and staff during and after disasters.

Things like, sustainment, collaboration, and continuation of services are covered in the plan.

While these assist us greatly in extending care and comfort to our patients and coordinating their welfare, a large part of our role in a post-disaster situation is simply providing reassurance and comfort.

Under normal conditions, Hospice brings together a team of people—medical, social workers, spiritual advisors, trained volunteers—who work with the person who is dying, the caregiver, and/or the family to provide the medical, emotional, and spiritual support needed. This can be heightened during and following a natural disaster.

The patient's physical needs are the first priority, maintaining their comfort and medical routines as closely as possible. This may require transfer to a facility, if the home has been compromised. However, the goal is to meet these immediate and short-term needs as quickly and seamlessly as possible.

The requirements of my job—professional skills, problem solving, and most especially, compassion, are even more important following a disaster, like Michael. Initially, I'm simply bearing witness to people's stories — providing them the space to share and process. Then, after the immediate shock is over, my focus shifts toward the short-term medical and emotional concerns, and finally to the longer-term effects of the trauma. For a variety of reasons, some people are able to rebuild and return to close to their "normal" functioning quite quickly. But for others, especially those with serious and terminal medical conditions or with limited access to services and support, the effects can linger long after the debris has been cleared. Addressing the long-term needs of my patients, ensuring they have access to the health and other resources needed is critical.

In my role, as a Hospice Social Worker, I assist the patient and their family in navigating the already intense challenges that come with serious illness or the-end-of-life-journey. During times of disaster, my services and continued compassionate support, become even more critical.

When people ask me about my job, I often tell them, "I do a little bit of everything. It changes day-to-day and patient to patient. I connect with my patients and their families in a very real and lasting way, bringing joy and peace when I can."

The challenges of serious and terminal illness can be daunting during the best of circumstances. In the days and weeks since Michael devastated the Florida Panhandle, the one thing I have found to be most effective has been helping my patients and their families escape the increased worry and anxiety the storm has caused. Even for just a little while.

I try to bring some kind of joy and laughter to every visit, to leave the patient and their family a bit lighter so they can better cope with what they are dealing with. In this respect, and especially during the daunting road we're now facing, I believe my role is a true calling. One I am so very honored to have received.

ELECTRICITY REQUIRED

by Linda Artman

For nearly 35 years, they had shared their lives. Families and friends had blended, as had vacations, possessions, happy times, and medical problems for each of them in turn. And now one of the biggest problems they had faced together was barreling toward them while the world watched and the two friends, both retired nurses, made crucial decisions.

Pat and Sandy shared a duplex many years ago, each young woman having her own place to live. When the landlord made new plans for the property, it forced a change for the young women as they worked on graduate degrees with limited financial resources. They decided it made sense to find a place they could share. It would make living expenses more economical. Thus, began a lifetime of moving together for jobs, opportunities, and, finally, retirement in Florida.

Sandy developed some nagging health problems that had slowed her down a bit, but she still managed to cook and bake for many lucky folks, go to her shop to do wood-working projects, and walk the dog multiple times each day. Pat contracted COPD and is limited greatly by her difficulty breathing and the constant need for supplemental oxygen. Going to church and playing bridge are her outlets.

Living in a mandatory evacuation zone made it clear that they should leave before Hurricane Michael came too close. The storm was growing so quickly, and the logistics of a hurried departure complete with many types of medical equipment, the dog and his needs, and the normal luggage necessary for a multiple-day trip, made for a pretty stressful experience.

"If I don't have electricity for my oxygen machine, I die," Pat stated matter-of-factly. It's that simple. And that important. And that unalterable.

Choosing a place to go where Michael wouldn't follow them was critical in their planning. Going somewhere that might also be without power could *not* happen. After careful consideration they left their condo, heading to Birmingham, AL. Tracks for Michael showed his projected path turning east, thus they felt they would be safe.

In Birmingham the news was anything but comforting. The storm was becoming a monster, and Pat and Sandy watched with growing concern for the home they had left behind. News from neighbors was impossible to get after the power went out and all communication was lost. So, they watched The Weather Channel and worried. A lot.

It took a couple of days for news to sift out of the quiet community that Sandy and Pat had left behind in Panama City. The TV showed such awful destruction in the whole area, but no personal news about their home and neighbors. *That's* what they needed to know about. *That's* what was in their thoughts constantly.

When news finally came that home and friends were safe, they decided to make their way closer to Panama City. Trees were down everywhere, and access would be blocked for some time. More importantly, there was no electricity. But being closer felt better. They would be able to get home sooner once the roads were clear and Pat's life would be protected by the return of steady power.

Miraculously, power was restored to Pat and Sandy's area a little more than a week after Michael blasted through leaving his calling card everywhere. They traveled toward Panama City at last. It was so good to get home and to be welcomed back into the safe enclave of their community. Areas all around theirs were virtually destroyed, but there was only minor damage done to their buildings along the bay. They were so grateful that all of their memories, represented by the artwork and treasures they had gathered over the years, were intact. They wouldn't have to begin again. It would have been so much more difficult with age and health issues.

Nearly all of the grand, old trees that were part of the sheltering appearance at the gate to their community were gone or broken, leaning at unnatural angles. The sight that welcomed them back was unfamiliar and missing the warmth and security that they hadn't even known they counted on to be a part of "home." Everyone was facing the same adjustments to the new landscape, even the dog seemed a bit unsure of things.

The neighborhood worked together to clean up the mess Michael left. Each did what he or she was able. Some used chainsaws and some stacked piles of branches. Some cleaned up miscellaneous debris and some brought iced tea. There was a community lunch provided by some who were unable to help with the heavy labor required. They were one. They cared about each other even more than before and they showed it in many ways.

When the air conditioning unit went out in Sandy and Pat's condo on a weekend night shortly after their return, it was a serious concern. The heat and stagnant air caused an emergency for Pat even with her oxygen machine. Neighbors brought fans and checked on them frequently. Plans were discussed for a move to a neighbor's home if things couldn't be rectified. Everyone was willing to do whatever it took to keep Pat safe. Fortunately, the A/C was repaired and both women, and their dog, were soon comfortable.

In the days and weeks that followed, it became ever clearer that Michael had brought a close-knit community even closer together out of shared concern for each other, individually *and* as a group.

TALK OF DEATH
by Sandi Klug-Lard

The red mark's still on so many houses in my neighborhood, like the lamb's blood smeared over the doorway so the Angel of Death would pass over.

I'll never forget stepping outside for the first time after the hurricane and seeing four trees on my neighbor's house and three cars in their driveway. We thought they were home. We screamed at the kids to stay inside as we called out for our neighbors and looked through the rubble, wholly expecting to see dead or broken bodies.

They had children, the thought ran through my head as I raced towards the house through the wreckage. I remember seeing them jumping out of that red car, now under a two-ton tree, after getting home from school.

They weren't home. Their home is an empty lot now, three months later.

We went to our elderly neighbors next. We screamed for them, too. We knew they had stayed, we had checked with them the night before. We pounded on the doors begging for them to answer.

"Sandi, their car isn't in the driveway."

"When did they leave, then?"

"I don't know."

Then, there they were. It took them two hours to find a way back home when they only went a mile away. They told us their story. At 4 a.m. they'd decided to leave and go to a friend's house, only to spend hours holding the French Doors of their friend's home closed against the wind. The doors were eventually ripped off the home as they sat there helplessly watching the storm whip around them.

They would have been better off at home, but how could they have known? Our other neighbors were better for leaving, but the ones standing before us would have been better off staying.

Jesse and I looked at each other. We always wanted to replace our sliding glass door with French Doors, but not anymore. At least we knew our doors were monster proof.

We heard a yell down the road, "HEY! ARE YOU OKAY DOWN THERE?!"

"ALL IS WELL!" My husband yelled back. "IS ANYONE INJURED?! I'M A MEDIC!"

"ALL IS WELL!" came the reply.

We gave the street one last look under that creepy orange sky, and that's when we heard them.

The helicopters.

Their spotlights highlighted us below, the dust-smoke made of broken pine trees cast a hazy mist around the light.

"This is something out of a movie," said my husband.

"Alarms in the background and everything," I replied. The elementary school's alarm lulled us to sleep that night.

"Shut up!" My husband yelled later into oblivion towards the helicopters. "Don't they know we're trying to sleep here?"

"I wonder what they must be thinking up there?" I replied.

"That we're all dead," said my husband, his last words before sleeping.

Today, I walked my kids to the park. The first time since the storm. We used to go all the time, but the debris still littering the streets and the stumps of trees blocking the sidewalks has kept us from our walks.

So many houses still bear this mark. This mark that simply means, "No one here is dead."

Red markings, like these, were placed by rescuers on properties to indicate they had been checked and cleared. *Photo by Sandi Klug-Lard*

The date of October still tattooed on our houses, lest we forget it. As though we could.

I see how my neighborhood used to look as a veil covering the present. I hear the songs of birds, the birds that don't sing anymore with no homes to live in. I even see the shadows of the trees covering the street as they once did, their own kind of veil from the heat of a blazing Floridian sun.

I see everything as it once was, so vividly I can almost ignore the destruction that truly lies beneath the confines of my imagination.

My heart breaks still, I can't help it. The red markings on the doors hold the reality we live in.

"No one here is dead." It doesn't feel like we're alive either.

The shops still empty, the ghosts of our favorite stores still haunt the sides of our highways. Most are still closed, some indefinitely.

And those red markings on the doors.

How do you pick up the pieces? How long is too long to grieve? How do you move forward when the red paint is still there, on the doorways, along with the debris, trash, broken fences, and lives still so plainly visible?

As if the storm only happened yesterday.

We've come so far with still so much distance to go. People are tired and strong. We still see everything through a veil of how it was, how it still could be.

I now know what people mean when you ask them how they are, and they reply, "I can't say." I know what it means to carry grief beyond words in your heart. I know what it means when people lie and say they're "fine" when they're not.

It's not because they want to lie, it's because they're tired of explaining the grief. When they speak of it they must relive it and it's exhausting.

I think I will know we've made progress when the red marks have been washed away. Or perhaps when my neighbor's house is a house again, not an empty lot. Or maybe when I see a hundred new fences and roofs.

I just don't know, but today was hard. I can see the progress and also the length of the distance still to travel. I can see I have new walls in my house and a roof, but I can also see the work left to be done.

And I have to live in it, every single day. A constant reminder of what is still lacking.

Or, what is just beginning.

I can still see the red marks on the doors. As if the Angel of Death put them there afterward and said, "I felt favorable towards your town today, so I passed over you."

I can only hope my grief will be as kind and pass over, too.

Opposite Page: Arity Wales Saltwatercolour and Acrylic on 16"x20" stretched canvas. "Fear not the depths. Life is the chisel, hammer, and storm. We are the icebergs in the seas of circumstance and fates. With each life event, we are weathered and chipped away, lightening our load to reveal the greater depths of our being. Fear not the depths for they can boast the most beautiful part of ourselves into an artful manifesto."

— Melinda Hall

Photo by Melinda Hall

IRONY

What do you call

A roofing company with no roof?

A homeowner with no home?

A beachfront property owner with no beachfront?

A student with no school?

Ironic? No. I call it home.

—Jennifer N. Fenwick, *December 31, 2018*

Photo by John Fenwick

GRACE IN THE FACE OF HURRICANE BRAIN

by Johanna Rucker

*The winds and the waves shall obey thy will. Peace, peace be
still. I'm not aware of feeling afraid.*

Because of inner guidance to live there, I moved from
Wilmington, Delaware, to the Eagles Landing Apartments on
Harrison Avenue in Panama City, Florida. I moved in January of 2018.
Nine Months later, Hurricane Michael hit.

My place wasn't in the area of an evacuation zone, so I hunkered
down in my apartment, well supplied with food, water, and batteries.
Luckily, just in case, I'd even taken "before" pictures of my newly
furnished home—for insurance purposes, you know.

The morning of October 10, I waited for the storm with calm
confidence and mild curiosity. At first, it just seemed like a pretty
strong storm. But then the winds picked up quickly and the wall of
my bedroom began to vibrate. Here we go.

I find myself in a narrow closet, crouched on a small file cabinet,
driven there by rattling walls, dripping ceiling, crashing glass. I'd
retreated to this last refuge when the bedroom ceiling caved in, after
the chimney crashed to the ground, after the wall over the fireplace
blew open, and a roaring wind invaded my living room—a deluge
over my new sofa and chair—as pictures crashed to the floor, after
windows shattered and shards of glass littered the carpet, as cottony
pink insulation plastered the walls and plugged the toilet with rosy
refuse.

Johanna's apartment before and after Michael. *Photo by Johanna Rucker*

I'm praying in the closet, wondering if its ceiling too will collapse. I'm chanting Om Mani Padme Hum, I'm calling on Jesus, Mary, and Joseph, on Saint Padre Pio, on Amma, the hugging Saint. I'm asking Archangel Michael and the angels of the storm to calm the roar—the whiteout so loud that even the splintering of trees can't be heard over its deafening sound. I sing to myself.

I'm not aware of feeling afraid.

Two hours and an eternity later, the storm quiets. I step out of the closet, cautious, picking my way over ceiling board and around piles of refuse—Searching out the eight others in my apartment building who have come through the mauling. All have survived without injury. That is grace.

Huddled outside among the detritus of our building, we stare in disbelief into what had so recently been a forest of stately pines—now a pathetic field of broken, bent, splintered limbs and trunks.

But I don't stick around.

I'm in a hurry. No time to chit chat about whose apartment had more damage. I've got to go. I am out of there. With a suitcase, the file cabinet of crucial papers, some food, and my cell phone, I head for my car. Somehow, I've managed to be clear minded enough to gather the essentials. That is grace.

After the storm, Johanna returned to her Panama City apartment to recover what items she could. She was greeted by friends who were happy to help her sift through her former life. *Photo by Jason Hedden*

Grace too in the fact that the trees near my car fell the opposite way. The car is banged up but drivable! Others tell me I can't get out, but I don't listen. Dodging downed trees, felled signs, light poles, and wires lying in the roads, driving through foot-deep puddles, I persist.

As I find myself on route 231 heading north for Interstate 10, I recognize nothing—no buildings, no signs, no landscapes. All are decimated. Driving with focused concentration, I somehow emerge from the debacle.

Now that's grace. There's even an open gas station by I-10. They can offer no gas or electricity, but I can pee and get directions to Tallahassee. The interstate is blocked to all but emergency vehicles, so I have to take a 2-hour detour. As I head north towards Dothan, Alabama, I notice with intense relief that fewer and fewer of the trees are cracked in half, and it's easier to navigate around the few still in the road.

Grace carries me east from Dothan along route 84 across South Georgia. Around Donaldsonville, trees are again down everywhere, and it's tough going. Desperate to relieve myself, I pull up behind a gas station whose canopy has crashed to the ground and pee next to my car. Desolation.

Yet my cell phone battery holds out and somehow T-Mobile comes through. I let friends know I am on my way. Grace, grace, grace. I get to my friends' home safe and sound—intact houses! Standing trees! Running water! Miracle upon miracle.

Now, three months later, grace accompanies me moment to moment as I begin to rebuild my life here in Tallahassee. I'm still disoriented, but at least safe here, and I have friends and a sense of community. Yet for me, as for thousands of others who were in its path, the storm goes on—we have "hurricane brain"—the white-out roar of 150-mile an hour winds still rushes through our nervous systems—our bodies have absorbed a cellular terror, as the trauma loops around within.

Waves of sorrow for my lost town wash through me—I sorrow for my friends who are still living under tarps, and for all those still homeless. Post traumatic STORM disorder accompanies my days, keeping my inner world in disarray.

And yet,—even now—grace abounds, as my empathy for the many experiencing such disruption increases, as my compassion for myself and each one affected grows daily. Even while the trauma is still very real to me, I am beginning to look for ways to give back, as grace in abundance accompanies me through this valley of the shadow of death.

WHERE CAN I REST NOW

I've created a reasonable facsimile of
my Panama City apartment—
the one the hurricane demolished—
here in Tallahassee.
But I know it's a fake.

It's nothing but a pathetic stage set—
A mere hologram of normalcy.

At any moment it could shimmer into
The mirage it truly is,
And desert me in the featureless space
That is where I am now.

The checks from Allstate insurance
Assure me that I can replace the missing pieces.
This is a terrible joke—
No confidence in a physical world can be bought
with Cold, Hard, Cash.

What has been blown to smithereens
In that fierce gale
Or ruined with mold
Is not the blue-jeans-blue sofa or the lime green chair,
So overstuffed and comfy,
But the idea that those bulky objects actually exist.

Where is the inner sofa?
I have no place to rest.
Where are the ceiling, the walls, of my inner house?
There is nowhere to shelter.
Where are inner food and drink?
No place to preserve, to store, to cook
To eat.

In this sheer, stark, empty plain,
Only a white board exists.
I can write poem words on that vast blank space,

Using a smelly red marker,
And in an instant, dry-erase those red marks from the white,
As the wind erased my Panama City life.

I can draw pictures—even pretty recognizable ones,
Of the Blue Sofa and the Green Chair.
And I can dry-erase them too,
In the twinkling of a swipe.

I can imagine a whole new life
In this new version of a
Two-bedroom, two-bath apartment,
With its new Blue sofa and loveseat—
With its new version of a bed,
Not a queen, but a full-size mattress.

I can ride around in a shiny new car,
So much nicer than the moldy oldy from the storm.

And in this different town,
I can reach out to different friends,
(Neither is a reasonable facsimile of
Any place or any one.)

Yet here, in this liminal bardo of unbecoming,
Neither original Blue nor new Blue sofa
Can give me a place to sit.

Where can I rest now?
Only in the seat of love.

        —Johanna Rucker, *November 14, 2018*

COWBOY COFFEE AND KINDNESS

by Linda Artman

Through the devastation Michael left behind, love and kindness would prove much stronger.

"I'm scared, Mom," her daughter admitted.

"I am, too," was Barbara's sincere response.

The morning that Michael arrived, Barbara and her daughter were in the yard talking as they watched their "dog cousins" run around. Barbara and her husband, Tom, were getting settled with the extended family gathered in their large home. An adult son works for the county and couldn't evacuate because he would be on-call as soon as the storm passed to help put the county infrastructure back together. Their son-in-law is a school principal and he needed to be in place, too. No way would the family split up, so they gathered with grandkids, dogs, and then increasing anxiety as Michael approached, becoming stronger and fiercer.

The power went out early, before Michael fully introduced himself. Then the wind blew, and the rain came. It got so strong and so loud that the whole family went into the "Man Cave," a room they deemed the safest place in the house.

When the first big tree blew down, they got a mattress to put over the one window in their safe room. It seemed like it went on forever. More big trees went down. It was loud. It was frightening.

When it was finally over, the family and the dogs went outside to find a whole new world. The big trees they'd heard fall were blocking everything. The backyard didn't even look familiar without the sheltering pines. Everything seemed bare and foreign. The road in front of the house was completely blocked with trees and debris. Before long there was an army of neighbors outside assessing the new landscape of the neighborhood, and then wielding chainsaws to alter it. It was a huge effort, made lighter by the willingness of each to help the other. Oh, and there was a tree resting on the roof, blocking a way to assess the damage. But that would wait.

The next morning the family got the grill going on the back porch and made a warm breakfast of bacon, eggs, and cowboy coffee. Barb and Tom took a share of the meal next door when they went to check on the elderly couple who counted on their help frequently in normal situations.

This morning found things worse than normal. The man had fallen on the way to the bathroom in the night and couldn't get himself off the floor. He'd been there for hours with his leg bent unnaturally beneath him. It took Tom *and* his son to get him in his bed. He was in terrible pain, and it was feared he was going into shock. Barb and her daughter went off in search of medical help. Phone lines were down, and cell service had been noticeably unavailable. It meant getting in Tom's big diesel truck and setting off around trees and other debris blocking the way.

Barb rode shotgun as her daughter maneuvered the large vehicle. They tried to find a nurse that they knew lived in a neighboring community, but found she had evacuated. EMS services were suspended, so they drove to the nearby fire station to ask for help. First responders from out of the area were on site and willing to make a trip to the house but couldn't promise how soon. A neighbor, who is a trauma nurse, came to offer her help; the ambulance arrived. All present agreed that the elderly couple were unable to care for themselves in the current conditions, and they were both transported to facilities in Pensacola. Neither wanted to leave their home, so Barbara and her daughter had to work hard to convince them it was the right thing to do.

Having no power, no water, and no internet made everything very difficult for the next few days. Gradually, all of these things returned, and with each one, life became easier. It gave Barb the ability to volunteer at the church distribution center. Tom spent hours working on the many fallen trees. The house and yard looked more orderly. Life was very different still, but one step at a time they were putting their home, family, and neighborhood back together.

After many shared meals, working cell phones, and stories, everyone finds it a closer-knit, warmer place to be. Michael brought strangers, neighbors, and families together through shared experience and working with each other for the betterment of all.

So many historical landmarks were destroyed by Hurricane Michael. This clock, which has marked the passage of time in the downtown area of Panama City since 1927, though damaged, survived the storm. *Photo by Jennifer N. Fenwick*

WHERE HAVE ALL THE TREES GONE?

Where have the trees all gone?
In this season, when trees are a
Symbol of new birth and life?
Oh. Yes, they were taken by the storm.
Torn from their growing places
Roots and limbs left exposed and bare.
Their branches bowed beneath
The force of the relentless wind.
Where have the trees all gone?
The ones left behind, lonely sigils
Over barren land, weeping at the loss.
Don't be discouraged, they whisper,
New life will come. See? My new leaves already sprouting?
In time, I will cast shadows and shade once more.
Until then, use my broken branches
Collect my withered limbs and upon
Their bows hang lights and holly.
Place your treasured globes upon
my naked wood and believe with me.
The sun will rise tomorrow, our Savior's
Blessed birth heralded by the dawn.

— Jennifer N. Fenwick, *December 12, 2018*

Under the Oaks, a popular park in the Callaway area, was decimated by Hurricane Michael. The majestic oak trees, that at one time provided ample shade, stripped bare by the damaging winds. *Photo by Ashley Davis*

FORGETTING AND
REMEMBERING

Let's see, October 10 to December 1,
How many days and weeks has it been—
What is the time-distance between me and
Hurricane Michael?

How many new memories have been laid down,
since the experience of
The chimney blowing off?
The gale sweeping the living room,
Rain, wind, horror bursting through,
Breaking windows—

The memory is still vivid,
But the numbness has worn off—
The dull Novocain ache
Giving way to whole body screams, racking soundless
sobs—pain that seemed my permanent life.

But now, Day 52, week 8,
Another kind of memory glimmers to the surface,
of when,
the night before the storm,
(October 9) I went with a new friend
To the Panama City Science and Discovery Center where we
Admired snakes, turtles and iguanas
In their terrariums
and heard an Audubon society talk on
environmental concerns
for the brown headed nuthatch
And then walked around downtown
And got a hoagie at the Funky Mermaid cafe.
Found 6 pennies on the sidewalk,
Which we shared, 3 each, between us for good luck and
friendship.

How peaceful and unaware we were
That the next morning the Science and Discovery Center
would lose its roof,
And the pine forests of the nuthatch would
Crack over,
And yet, I hear, the terrariums held strong,
And the snakes, turtles, and iguanas were safe
In their human habitat.

Little did we know that the downtown streets
Where we strolled would be littered with bits of roof, wire,
and shattered glass,
And the big square clock that had hung at the corner of
Harrison and Fourth would lie surrendered on its side
Hands stopped at the awakening numbers—11:11.

But now, Day 52, the memories of what my life was before
the storm begin to emerge—
A slow sunrise,
The surprise of sunbeam,
Piercing a dense dark gloom.

I still have my three pennies,
And my friend has brought his.
We are alive and laying down new memories
In the town to which I fled.

— Johanna Rucker, *December 1, 2018*

SIDE BY SIDE

Every weekend they visited
these springs, paddling their kayak
in and out of moss leaden groves
capturing the wonder on film,
nestling it firmly in their hearts.

They rejoiced in the simplicity.
This masterpiece hand-crafted
by nature, marvelling that something
so majestic existed,
right outside their door.

They treasured these moments.
This communion with nature
and the magic living,
breathing all around them.

But that was before.
Before nature wrought
a different kind of fury.
Before everything changed.
In the blink of an eye,
their magic was altered.
Its past destroyed.

Side by side they witness
the changes
the beauty lost
the destruction left behind.

But what of the other destruction?
The one existing bone deep?
The one they carry inside them?
The one that remembers,
and now must go on.

— Jennifer N. Fenwick, *January 8, 2019*

Before and after photographs of some of the Springs located in the Panhandle of Florida. It will be years before the lush greenery returns and the Springs regain their pre-storm beauty. *Photo by Jason Davis*

THE COMFORT STATION
by Linda Artman

"They're hiring nurses right now for the county Comfort Stations," a friend told 25-year-old Brooke.

She had recently finished her nursing education and had been looking for a job. There had been an interview scheduled at one of the local hospitals—But Hurricane Michael had gotten there first. The hospital was badly damaged, and all patients and services had been evacuated and transferred to other facilities. It would be awhile before any job search could happen there.

Brooke's experience through the storm had really shaken her. She and her young son had originally taken shelter at her mom's house in Lynn Haven. As the storm strengthened, her mom had had a bad feeling about things, and they had all decided to go to Geneva, Al, where her dad lives. She had felt so frightened and helpless.

Watching Michael's progress had been additionally stressful because she was worried about her son's father, who was hunkered down in a bathroom in Southport the last time she had heard from him. He was worried about their son, too. They had seen such frightening posts and videos on Facebook and the internet before power was lost, and then they were unable to communicate at all.

Imagination can take complete control of one's mind, and they were both suffering from just that problem. They were shocked at what they had seen and heard about the strength of the storm. They went 24 long hours without any communication, despite many futile attempts. *Finally,* a borrowed phone with working service gave comfort to each knowing that they had all made it through the horror of Michael's fury. Such incredible relief—

Two days after Michael blew out of Lynn Haven, Brooke went back. Trying to find Mike, her son's father, was a frustrating and time-consuming task. They still had no way to communicate save "old school" leaving of notes with time hacks and intended next steps. It took several iterations before they finally found each other.

The sights that confronted them were so shocking that they didn't seem real. Brooke couldn't even feel any emotion at first. Then she discovered that she was afraid in her new surroundings. There were looters making their way in neighborhoods that had never before seen such activity. She kept her gun close to her for security. After getting some clothes and other belongings, she headed back to Alabama and safety.

There, reality set in. Hard. How would she pay her bills and take care of her son? The hospital was gone as was the job opportunity she had counted on to set their future. She was safe in Alabama away from the destruction and heartache back in Florida—and felt guilty for that. She felt totally adrift and helpless.

Hearing about the Comfort Station job openings was just what she needed. And the county didn't know it yet, but she was just what they needed! Neither Brooke nor the folks who hired her had any idea how the next few weeks would change her life and the lives of many others.

Brooke found the large white tent set up in a park in a particularly hard-hit area in an old part of town. The houses are old, small, and close together. Nearly every house was damaged. Badly. Trees were in or on most of them. The destruction was almost complete. Entering the tent set up on wet ground, Brooke was sobered even further. Her "office" was bare. There were a couple of long tables set up, a few folding chairs, and a package of paper towels. There was no food, no water, and no medical supplies.

Displaced and homeless residents take advantage of the comfort stations and supply tents that were established throughout the storm-battered region. For some, it was their only means of rest, meals, and even hygiene in the weeks following Michael. *Photo by Linda Artman*

The first person to come to Brooke at the giant, empty tent was a rain-soaked woman who was chilled to the bone and starving. She had walked to the point of complete exhaustion to get help. Brooke went to get the only supplies she had—from her car and whatever was in it. She used her own medical equipment to get the woman's vital signs, gave her some food and her favorite jacket, used her yoga mat to make a pallet on the ground, and settled the completely spent woman down to rest. It became obvious just how tired her patient was—She slept for seven hours on the hard ground.

More people began to come to the tent for help. There were now showers and restroom facilities on site. Little by little, water and food began to arrive for distribution. On Day 3 of her new job, a group called *The Sonder Project* came with people to help organize the large amounts of food, water, and medical supplies they unloaded from their truck. Brooke shared the excitement and gratitude of the neighborhood.

Becoming accomplished at networking, Brooke found ways to get the supplies people needed. Word spread, and more contributions found their way to the previously desolate tent. There was a steady stream of goods into and out of the tent, largely because of Brooke's procurement efforts and organizational abilities. Soon the county hired some help, and others volunteered in the Station. People from the surrounding area came in a steady stream searching for comfort and needed supplies. Many came with tears as they told their stories—and left with tears of gratitude at receiving evidence that others cared about their plight.

No one cared more than Brooke.

She gave a warm personal welcome to each person who entered. She treated everyone with dignity as she asked quietly if they needed personal items—like underwear, feminine hygiene products, or adult diapers. She treated everyone with concern and respect. There were also a few times that Brooke had to get tough to keep things fair and orderly. She did that, too.

Gratitude came in the form of thank you's and lots of hugs, heartfelt and often accompanied by tears. Seeing the relief in parents' eyes as they saw an immediate and concrete way to meet the basic needs of the family—for today—touched a chord in Brooke. She had recently shared those feelings as she accepted *this* job at *this* place. Futures were unsettled and uncertain for all of them. She totally understood.

"In doing this job, I learned a lot. I am honored to have helped. It really reeled things in for me. I know that we don't really need to go back to normal. Some of this is better. An experience like this really humbles you."

BROKEN

Broken fences

Discarded trees

No longer standing

No longer shading

So much lost

So much revealed

The only certainty left?

We'd never be the same.

Within the destruction

Lay our rebuilding

Within the chaos

Lay our growing

Within the heartache

Lay our healing.

— Jennifer N. Fenwick, *December 24, 2018*

Timber damage in the region is estimated at 1.3 billion. "This is a catastrophic loss to the forest industry in the Florida Panhandle," said Florida Commissioner of Agriculture, Adam H. Putnam. "We are committed to helping Florida recover from this devastating storm and will continue to work closely with the agriculture industry on hurricane-related damage assessments." (reported by WJHG/WECP, October 19, 2018) *Photo by David Herring/ Shutterstock*

A GRIM REALITY LIVES HERE

by Erica McNabb Floyd

A grim reality lives here. It collects in puddles of sadness from all the tears falling from the gray skies. Dying dreams hang on the broken limbs of trees that once stood tall and proud, such as we are. Where we once heard the wind through the pines like a child's lullaby, is now the crisp sound of the blue cover flapping like wings of dragons that may swoop down at any given time to consume us.

I remember the lush green grass that once cushioned my bare feet and how I thought it would be here forever. It feels like that memory is being drowned with each raindrop that falls.

The sounds of all the birds announcing their busy day has long been replaced with the sounds of emptiness and screams of despair. Or maybe no one hears the screams. Are those sounds only heard in my own mind? I can't seem to hear over the deafening silence.

Every day when I step outside my eyes tell me progress is being made, but my heart and mind tell me we are mourning a loss. A funeral of sorts. Mourning and grieving the loss of the beauty of the land, of normality, of a life we once knew. Except there are always beautiful flowers at funerals and I can't seem to find any here.

One day the swamp of sadness will be but a memory, a chapter in the book that is my life. But for today the grim reality resides right here with me with no plans of leaving anytime soon.

Miles of storm debris lined streets in the region for weeks. In the first three months following Michael, twenty years of debris was removed. Clean-up is ongoing. *Photo by David Herring/Shutterstock*

THREE UNFORGOTTEN MILES

They celebrated there.
Birthdays. Graduations.
Their parent's 40th Anniversary.
It's gone now. The Fish House.
Like everything else on that beach.
Like their dad, who passed
a few months after they'd
celebrated he and mom's 50th.

They rode there.
On Saturday mornings
On the Harley she'd surprised
him with for his birthday.
Windblown and laughing,
they'd always stop in.
To grab a bite.
For the friendly welcome.
It's gone now too,
Sharon's Cafe. Another
casualty of that day.

They walked hand-in-hand
on the public pier.
Watching sunsets.
Falling in love.
He proposed there.
On one knee.
Tears in her eyes.
She said yes.
That was ten years ago.
They're still going strong,
though the pier,
where it all started,
no longer stands.
Some things remain sturdy
in memory only.

The Forgotten Coast it's called.

Unmarred by commerce.
Quaint.
Charming.
Pristine.
Ground Zero they call it now.
The epicentre.
Obliterated.
War zone.
Devastated.

Mexico Beach Strong.
Spray painted on debris.
On remains of buildings.
On upturned sidewalks.
Three miles of unforgettable coast.
Three miles of unforgettable strength.
Three miles of unforgettable determination.
Three miles. It seems so much farther now.

— Jennifer N. Fenwick, *January 11, 2019*

Storm ravaged Mexico Beach bore the brunt of Michael's intense fury. The three-mile stretch of coastline will never be the same. *Photo by Terry Kelly/Shutterstock*

REFLECTIONS FROM A VOLUNTEER

by Linda Artman

November 3, 2018—It's been almost a month since Michael roared through. We have power and water, but some still don't. There will be piles of giant cut-down trees higher than the houses behind them for months as the trucks rumble through every street in every community trying to clean up.

Added to the roadside piles are couches, beds, clothing and anything else that got wet and is molding and useless. The piles of insulation, wood, broken windows, roofing, sheetrock, and unidentifiable pieces of houses are everywhere. The electric and cable linemen are still trying to connect us all with electricity, phone, cable, and internet. Even in areas where all of that has been restored, there are sporadic problems and/or temporary outages. Wires still lay on the ground or dangle from poles or tree limbs. There are miles of lines still on the ground, crossing roads, on sidewalks, and in yards.

I've been volunteering every day since I got here. For 2 days I helped an organization called *Mercy Chefs*. (A very worthy non-profit that goes wherever there has been a disaster to help in the immediate aftermath with feeding and caring for the people affected.) I helped the staff and volunteers make and serve over 1,000 people at each meal. The last day was Wednesday and we cleaned and broke down the site in a church parking lot.

The remains of a home amidst piles of debris. *Photo by Linda Artman*

Many of their staff had not been home for more than 2 months as they followed flooding in TX, then helped with Hurricane Florence in NC, before coming to Panama City. They were tired but full of positivity and love for the opportunity to help where it was so desperately needed.

The next two days I worked at a distribution center at a local church. They gave up their entire children's building to become a warehouse. They organized an amazing system of packaging food, hygiene items, cleaning supplies, tools, flashlights, baby food, formula, diapers and wipes, and so much more—And then they found a way to treat each person with dignity as they made special requests for additional needs. The system they devised was inspired. I helped package items, helped "shop" for the folks who came hour after hour, loaded cars, and began packing up for moving to the church's on-going food pantry mission. They will cease operations as a distribution center at the end of today's session, and the children will be able to reclaim their space.

I will load my car on Monday morning and take a load of supplies to a church in Port St Joe—on the other side of the Mexico Beach you heard so much about on the news. We may not be allowed to go through the area, which will add miles to the already 80-mile round trip exercise.

There were so many sad stories as we visited with people needing help. I found out about a part of town where it's been difficult to get supplies and most there have disabled vehicles and can't get out to get anything. So many fallen trees and structures destroyed the ability to go even short distances to take care of basic needs. The distribution church is taking a truck in there and I will probably go there to help on Tuesday.

The landscape is forever changed. I've gotten lost trying to go somewhere because all of the landmarks and street signs are gone. The people I've met and worked with, as well as the people so profoundly affected by loss, are changed, too. Most are changed for the better—or will be when they can get out of survival mode, breathe, and see the ways people cared and helped. Caring and helping each other is everywhere. Piled higher than the debris.

Gratitude is palpable. I'm so proud to be part of this area. It is special—especially in its suffering.

November 5, 2018—On Monday I drove a load of supplies through Mexico Beach. I'm not posting pictures from there because I had to keep driving in the long lines of giant debris removal trucks. I thought I'd seen enough pictures to understand and be prepared for what I'd see there. I wasn't. Not even close. There are no pictures and absolutely no words capable of doing that. It breaks my heart. And I will never be able to unsee the things I saw. If I lived to be 1000.

Yesterday I worked at a distribution center my friend and I found in an especially hard-hit area. The problem with that center was that there was almost nothing to "distribute." We went to Woodlawn United Methodist Church (the distribution center I worked at last week) and got as much as our 2 vehicles could hold. When we returned, we got a list of other needed items. A trip to the store gathered most of them, with a return to the store today to get the rest.

I bought the requested underwear in every size and kind imaginable. It was placed in a special area overseen by the amazing young nurse who has been hired to do a bit of everything needed. Before we finished unloading the SUV, a young mother was getting underwear for her children and herself.

Brooke, the young nurse, had discreetly asked if they needed underwear. They picked out a package of new, clean underwear each with such joy you would think it something incredible. The mother turned to me with tears in her eyes and said a quiet, heartfelt thank you. That's why I go back. Why I find a reserve of energy to call upon to get through more loading and unloading—of things heavy and light—than I've done in the last five years of my life!

The tandem trucks like the one in the picture are EVERYWHERE. It's such a good feeling seeing them because it means someone down that road won't have to look at a giant pile of debris another day.

The cut-up trees are taken to one of several designated areas where they are run through industrial chippers. The pile of mulch is growing rapidly at each one. Bulldozers push things around for efficiency and to keep the wood stirred so it won't heat up and spontaneously combust. Passing there, you can't help but notice the wonderful smell of pine—

Today I'm regrouping. Tomorrow I'll be back at the center hoping to find things to distribute. I hope to load my vehicle and drive through the neighborhood to deliver to those unable to get out to pick up what they need.

With miles of debris, the sight of tandem trucks like this one entering the area are a welcome sight. *Photo by Linda Artman*

November 10, 2018—And the devastation is STILL so real—Many are kind of shell-shocked. There's no end in sight. The nightmare is all around, and there's just no way to awake from it. The piles get larger as people discover more ruined, moldy parts of their homes, clothing, furniture. Everything. Every. Thing.

I'm still going to the Millville center, helping as much as I can. Lowe's will be delivering next week. Publix lets me come at 9:30 at night to take the bread and baked goods that didn't sell that day. I take it to Millville in the morning.

A friend spent days making cookies, brownies and pound cake. The smiles that shone on a cloudy, rainy morning when such treats were discovered on the table of necessities lit up that tent like nothing else could. Squeals of delight made my heart smile.

One of the volunteers comes every day to help even though she lost her house. The bread bakers at Publix, both have badly damaged homes. They ask for nothing for themselves, say they are so glad to have jobs and are anxious to hear about how the baked goods are received—happy to be helping others.

A wonderful man made and donated 22 quilts because he's worried about how the colder weather will affect people with holes in their homes. Quilting is what he does. Giving to others is who he is.

A local restaurant owner fed thousands of people free breakfast for 4 hours every day for 2 weeks. Volunteers helped bus tables, so they could accommodate the folks who came in hungry and left with full bellies and warm hearts. Amazing.

She's going to have free Thanksgiving dinner for the workers from all over the country here to help us—since they can't be home with their own families for the holiday.

At that same restaurant is a server who is a dental hygienist. Her old job is gone. She is so happy to be working in this place of love and support—and her smile shows it. She's proud and uplifted to be working with a staff that cares about each other and lets that overflow to strangers who need it.

A job fair was held in the parking lot of the badly damaged Panama City Mall on Friday. There was food and music there on Thursday to give the community a chance to be together for a bit of something besides survival.

There is still need. So much need. But here in the Florida Panhandle, there is also hope. There is such a shared sense of caring and helping despite—or maybe because of—personal loss. My heart swells with pride as the tears run down my cheeks.

A Job Fair held in the parking lot of the now closed Panama City Mall. *Photo by Linda Artman*

BRAND NEW DAY

When I awoke this morning
I paused for just a moment
And simply breathed.
Standing on the precipice
As a new day dawned
The sun lengthened
Illuminating my altered world.
The piles of debris still growing
As they wait patiently at the curb
Blue tarps on my roof keeping time
with Stars and Stripes on my porch
Each sounding a different melody
As they sway in the day's first breeze
Birds joining in their chorus
Broken branches a solemn stage
For their cheerful antics.
My eyes found clarity in the growing light
My racing mind stilled
My heartbeat slowed
I breathed another grateful breath.
I am here, the dawn seemed to say,
I will return again tomorrow.
And with a thankful nod,
I stepped into the brand-new day.

—Jennifer N. Fenwick, *November 24, 2018*

"MAJOR" RESPONSE

by Linda Artman

As with many things in this life, it all starts at home.

Major Otis Childs is the head of the local Salvation Army—with his wife working at his side. When they retire this summer, they will have a combined total 92 years of service in "The Army," as he referred to it during our interview.

You can bet that they have had many experiences in that time that have given them a strength of purpose and of faith with which to handle the effects of Hurricane Michael. The community has truly benefited from that. Major Childs' calm, kind, and gentle voice is significant to his leadership before, during, and after the near category 5 hurricane made a very personal appearance in the Florida Panhandle.

The Salvation Army response to every disaster follows a general plan with specifics added according to the requirements dictated by circumstances. Initially, the response begins in the local area and then moves out as needed, like ripples on a pond.

According to Major Childs, the first step in preparing for Michael's arrival involved getting all local recovery equipment and supplies staged safely out of the projected path of the storm. If they are damaged or destroyed, they are useless. The logistics of accomplishing that, with a fast-moving storm like Michael, started the whole process with a bit of tension and a deep sense of responsibility to get it right.

Both Major Childs and his wife, also Major Childs, moved into the Emergency Operations Center (EOC) before Michael started blowing things down. They stayed around the clock until it was safe to extend the response into the community. The days in the EOC were spent in the company of other first responders who worked together day and night, each contributing expertise in specific areas, combining knowledge and skills to achieve the most beneficial result for the devastated community.

"Having everyone under one roof, immediately accessible to each other, was invaluable," the Major shared. "We could actually send the first teams to specific addresses where needs were greatest."

After the initial 2-3 days of living at the EOC, the Childs' and others began assisting with the assessment of the area, determining a priority for response. Most of the Salvation Army buildings were damaged, and at least one was destroyed. One of the first tasks was to repair the damaged warehouse which would be needed to receive the myriad supplies and donations which would begin pouring in very quickly. Assessing what and where things were most needed, was a critical and very fluid process.

The needs were so great. The Salvation Army has a three-pronged general plan for their response. Hydration, nutrition, and spiritual needs are always addressed. Accomplishing that comes with the help of thousands of volunteers, donations, and incredible planning. The ripple effect, remember?

Teams came from all over Florida, then other Southern States, then from as far as Canada and Bermuda. They rotated in and out, staying for about two weeks. There were thirty mobile units supplied with meals from a central "kitchen" set up in tents on the old K-mart parking lot at the foot of the Hathaway Bridge. Before dawn each day the preparation for thousands of meals began, sending amazing aromas through the early morning air. Once the meals were ready, it was an organized ballet of vehicles entering, loading, and departing with nourishment for so many who were unable to provide even that basic human need for themselves and their families.

Each mobile unit comes to the area with all the supplies and equipment needed to be autonomous, except for the lifeline of meals delivered to each site daily. Many of those units proudly display signs bearing the names of other places they have served. It is a geography lesson of disasters—and humbling to realize how many have been helped when they needed it most.

With nine counties to serve, many of which were profoundly affected by Michael, the task was arduous. The incident teams heading up the overall response also rotated in and out every two weeks. There were daily conference calls–using the lone AT&T cell phone—with the out-of-area leadership of the Salvation Army. Major Childs described the difficulties that even that brought. The rest of the group was never really certain that the Panama City folks were even still on the call. The daily reports of how many meals and other supplies were distributed at each location were used during these calls to determine where and how they could be most effective with their outreach. Even with all the obstacles present, goals were met, and thousands were helped.

Major Childs explained that the central ingredient to the overall response in helping the Panhandle was cooperation. Police, Fire and Rescue, Medical, and thousands of volunteers worked together unselfishly and without staking out territories. It was a unified effort, coming from a position of concern and caring. It worked. Immediate needs were met, and the community drew together in the process.

Now, eight weeks after the awful storm, the Salvation Army has shifted its response.

People are currently faced with overwhelming and all–consuming problems related to restructuring their homes and their lives. There is often help available, but navigating the system of insurance, government, and private applications for payments or loans is daunting under the best of circumstances. These are far from the best of circumstances, and many just don't know where to turn. The Salvation Army is once again ready to help. There are long-term recovery groups being formed to help with everything from how to apply for help to counseling. Mental and emotional health are often ignored during the toughest times—only to resurface in sometimes unexpected ways. Helping with that is part of the Salvation Army's spiritual outreach plan, too.

A simple conversation with Major Childs is informative, comforting, and inspiring. There is no doubt that he cares about those he serves. Because he has been a part of many responses through his years of service, it is clear that he has an in-depth knowledge of how the organization works best and how to engage within the community to get things done.

Linemen from all over the country arrived on scene within days of the storm. Restoring power was a monstrous undertaking as power poles and lines were decimated by the 155-mph winds. *Photo by Brandon Perdue/iStock*

WE'RE ALL STORYTELLERS NOW

by Tony Simmons, reprinted by permission from The News Herald

They brought me their stories. Alone or as couples and occasionally in family units, they found my table and began to tell me what happened to them in the storm and how they've been coping in the aftermath.

There was the young woman who lived in a mobile home where she grew up, telling how she spent the early part of the storm consoling her husband, who wasn't from Florida and had never before experienced a hurricane. These noises and wind-shaking vibrations were normal, she said — until she started hearing noises and feeling shudders that she'd never heard during a storm. And then the first of the trees crashed through the roof, smashing into the bed where her husband had just minutes earlier been lying beside her. They were driven from the broken trailer into their car, then into the home of a neighbor.

A retired couple couldn't find a place to live while their home was under repair. They went door-to-door through Panama City Beach, checking condos and rentals. One location took their contact information and called them a couple of days later when a long-term space became available; a Canadian snowbird had canceled his reservation, not wishing to visit while the county was in hurricane recovery mode.

There was a family who had lost most of their belongings and wanted to talk about books, then segued into the arguments they had with contractors who tried to take shortcuts on their home repairs.

And a retired teacher whose face and eyes turned red at the memory of the storm. Of the neighbor's fence that smacked into his back porch and helped the wind rip away part of his roof.

— A gentleman in a hat and duster with his wife, a video producer, who shared their misgivings about evacuating, and how her father was so adamant about staying that they all stayed. "Next time, we'll tell him we're going on vacation," she said.

— A couple encouraging me to join a civic group, or failing that, to promote fundraisers for local schools — in particular, the Bay High School band's need to replace its destroyed instruments and uniforms.

A mother beaming with pride for her daughter, a young adult now, who is using her contacts and training to organize such a fundraiser.

— A woman with tears in her eyes as she talked about losing so many of the trees in her historic neighborhood and how it would never be the same, ever, for the rest of her days.

I confess that, when I first became aware the storytellers had found me and were coming my way, I wondered if I was prepared to receive them. I, too, have stories, and it isn't always easy to focus on another's words when those very words jar loose a whirl of images and emotions. They would start to speak, and their tale would bring my own experiences back to life. The roar of wind in my memory threatened to overshadow the rush of emotions they were sharing.

But I could see in their eyes the same haunted look I'd found just about everywhere in these recent weeks. Some people surround that look with anger or sarcasm, laughter or tears. Some try to hide it. Some, perhaps most disturbing, don't seem to be haunted at all.

Since Hurricane Michael changed our world, we've been awash in one another's stories. Like priests in a confessional booth or counselors in a comfortable chair, we are bound to listen, to empathize, to offer comfort when we can. Peace.

Tony Simmons is a writer and editor for The News Herald. His column appears weekly in the Entertainer.

OUR AFTER

We long for before.

Because this is our after.

We long for tomorrow.

Because this is our now.

We long for hope.

Because this is despair.

We long for healing.

Because this is destruction.

—Jennifer N. Fenwick, *January 9, 2019*

The marina in downtown Panama City was decimated by the more than 150-mph winds and widespread flooding Michael inflicted on the region. *Photo by Jack Hamm*

OUR NEW NORMAL
by Kristi Kirkland

I have always been one that prefers to see the beauty in everything. After all, that is a much better way to look at things — it is so much less stressful.

I know everyone is either still shell shocked or running around like crazy people trying to navigate our new norm.

I have to say in all this I have had some of my highest highs and lowest lows. I have cried more in the past week than my entire life for my community.

It is a strange place we all find ourselves in. You always think you know how you will act during a crisis/disaster but until it happens, we just really don't know how we will deal or what part of our personality will come to the surface. We all hope we will rise to the occasion, but the truth of the matter is we are all fragile, and well—human.

But, when you look at the destruction, the lost and desperate looks in the eyes of your neighbors, and see a foreign landscape in a place you knew like the back of your hand. How does one keep seeing beauty?

I tell you I see beauty now more than ever before. It is powerful and everywhere.

Yes, there is and will always be heartache, damage, loss, and pain. It is everywhere, and we would have to be blind to not see it—but to focus on that can literally lock you down in reverse.

When I look at the once proud and beautiful tree that stood like a sentinel in front of my home—that is now broken, tattered, and damaged beyond saving—I see beauty as it saved my home and I can only give thanks instead of mourning the loss. We will plant more!

When I look at my once bustling and beautiful community thinking back to being in long lines to get to work—I have to ask myself did I once look into the vehicle next to me? The beauty I now see is in all the windows rolled down no matter the weather. Seeing people waving to everyone, offering help, handing bottles of water out those once rolled up windows. Strangers are now neighbors and the last case of water we give out means as much to the giver AND the receiver. We will rebuild better!

Think back on how many times we walked through a store not greeting a soul; ate in silence at a restaurant; came home and vegged out in front of the TV; spent most of our weekends entertaining ourselves; saw a pet wondering down the road not giving it a second thought; witnessed sadness, but looked the other way; went months or longer without talking to our neighbors; heard a need and figured there's surely someone already helping; saw a plea for assistance on social media and kept scrolling; had the ability to offer a company discount but decided against it after running the 'numbers'; and so many other actions that marked our previous numbed normal existence.

Now, in our new norm, we greet everyone! Honk to show thanks to linemen and first responders; share our table at a restaurant because it is the only one open and there's a line; come home and check in with neighbors to see if they need anything; spend our weekends volunteering and helping others; see a pet wondering and bring them home until their family is found; witness sadness and reach out to help, even if it is just a hug; hear a need and immediately offer help along with the other dozen responding; see a plea on social media and not only share, but offer assistance; have the ability to offer a discount but instead choose to give 150 meals for free—offer free tire repairs—not charge for the cases of water in your store—buy dozens of pizzas and take them to a neighborhood—share your generator instead of powering only your needs—pull into a Wendy's parking lot just to pay for the meals of the Army reserves deployed here—check on a customer needing pest control and cut a tree down while you are there—help with an inspection and take the trash when you leave because you have the means to dispose of it—drive to another town in your community just to see if anyone needs help—buy a case of water for your family and 6 more to hand out on the way home. THIS I have seen, and done, and so much more it brings me to my knees, tears streaming down my face, and heart swelling like the grinch on Christmas growing three sizes bigger! We WILL come out on the other side stronger and better.

So yes, there is sadness, pain, and destruction—but there is so much more giving, healing, rebuilding, supporting, and yes so much more BEAUTY in our little community that has grown three sizes bigger from the support we are receiving and the locals becoming true neighbors and real friends. Would I wish this on anyone for the outcome we are now benefiting from—no, but it is here, and we are becoming a better community because of it.

Sunrise on a broken community. *Photo by Jennifer N. Fenwick*

ROUGH ROAD AHEAD

Rough road ahead.
Marks the beginning.
This road so unlike
Those that came before.
Nothing prepares you
For the scene that meets the eye.
Nothing equips you
For the shortness of breath,
The bone-deep heartbreak.
This road leads to the center.
The eye passed over here.
Ground zero it's called.
For miles it continues.
For miles it radiates outward.
Destructive ripples of a shattering
So thoroughly complete,
So devastating and present.
Rough road ahead.
Miles of carnage to travel.
Miles of broken to heal.
Miles of agony to withstand.
Miles of desolation to rebuild.
Rough road ahead
Marks the beginning.
But where, please tell me,
where is the end?

—Jennifer N. Fenwick, *January 10, 2019*

Jennifer N. Fenwick

This sign, marking the entry point to Mexico Beach, FL, signifies more than just the condition of the physical roads ahead for the people of the Panhandle. *Photo by Tony Miller*

181

WHAT WAS ASKED, WHAT WAS GIVEN
by Jared Brooks

It's been a little over 3 months since Hurricane Michael destroyed our lives here in the Panhandle. I don't think I ever posted any pictures of that day mainly because we were huddled in the bathroom during the height of the storm. I have included some of the pictures as a reminder of what we went through.

What did Michael do you ask?

Precious lives were lost and a lot of people just up and left. I can't say I blame them. My wife, Laura, and I have thought about doing just that many times, but we just can't bring ourselves to do it.

We still have debris piles larger than most houses. We have debris trucks running 7-days a week for at least 12-hours a day. And it doesn't look like they have made a dent, though we know they have.

We are living in houses that are missing roofs, missing siding, missing windows, flooring, walls, appliances, and much more. That is if we are not displaced from our home and living in a camper or miles away from our job and living in temporary housing.

Most of us have lost our church buildings and along with them countless memories. We have lost jobs, incomes, and any sense of normalcy. For those that are fortunate to still have a job, we sit in traffic that seems endless. What should take 20-minutes now takes an hour, if you're lucky.

Schools are still combined with other schools and teachers are trying to comfort children and teach them, all while trying to hold their own lives together.

We have lost countless trees and I now find myself saying, "I sure do miss that tree that use to be in my yard; at least we had some shade from it."

We have lost places where we love to eat, shop, boat, play, and spend our down time in. Some of those places will come back, others won't.

The damage just outside Jared and Laura Brook's Panama City home just after Michael passed was overwhelming. *Photo by Jared Brooks*

So, what has Michael given?

A new reality. A new appreciation for life.

I get to wake up every day because God chose to spare my life during the storm. I get to spend more time with my family because we don't have cable and internet. Neighbors continue to help neighbors. Strangers continue to help strangers. I was spared for a reason. I have a purpose in this life and that purpose is to love God and love others.

Before Michael I can honestly say that loving others was difficult. I didn't get up every day and thank God for the little things, but I do now. I still have a home to live in. No, it's not perfect and yes, it might have to be totally redone or knocked down, but I have a warm place to lay my head at night.

I certainly don't go hungry because God has blessed me with a job that provides income for my family. I have 2 amazing children that I love. Yes, they aggravate me and drive me crazy at times, but I love them, and they are so special. God has big plans for both of them.

I have the most amazing wife. Not only is she drop dead gorgeous, but she is a wonderful person and someone that I am fortunate to be spending my life with. She is an awesome mother to our children.

I have 2 parents that I love, and I know they love me. My dad works harder than any person I know, and my mom is a fighter. She is going through cancer treatments currently and will be at the University of Alabama, Birmingham (UAB) for at least the next month. But she is doing great and is in full remission. I have a brother, and though we live different lives, I know he loves me, and my family and we love him. He has a great heart and will do anything to help others.

So, Michael took a lot away from me, my family, and my community, but we are stronger than the winds. We are stronger than the waves. We will prevail. Thank you, Lord, for every day that you have blessed us with and help us to never forget what you have done for us.

Flooding, downed trees, powerlines, and destroyed homes marked the Brook's once tranquil neighborhood.
Photo by Jared Brooks

CRUSHED

Crushed.
The weight of the world
Across weary shoulders.
When did this load
Get so heavy?
How did all this brokenness
Come to be?
When will it ease?
This burden carried
Since that day?
How will this story end?
For it will.
That's how stories are.
Just, please tell me,
that we're strong enough
to write a happy ending?

—Jennifer N. Fenwick, *January 12, 2019*

Crushed. *Photo by John Fenwick*

HEALING THROUGH DARKNESS

by Heather Clements

It's been almost 3 months since the hurricane, and it's been more than difficult. I had worked all weekend and was looking forward to van camping the following weekend. My love for camping in the woods had recently been renewed and it was what I looked forward to most.

On Sunday, my husband, Mat, and I installed a new floor for the *CityArts Cooperative* kitchenette. The old floor had missing pieces and was just old and kind of gross looking, so the new faux wood vinyl floor was quite the contrast. It was a small thing, but it felt like a big difference and was an improvement.

Monday morning, October 8th, I was doing some work at *CityArts* while Mat's coffee shop was open. Regulars sipped coffee and talked a little of some hurricane on the way. It was the first either of us had heard about it, and it was supposed to arrive in 2 days.

This had become a routine; every summer there were hurricanes that might hit us; and every time the news seemed set on scaring us, causing panic, over-preparations, and then an anticlimactic event as we slept through minor rain or winds. At this point, hurricane hype was just that—hype. An annoyance. Another way for the media to spike their ratings. Talk of school closings made me roll my eyes and wonder what Madeline would do during the day off from high school.

Suddenly, there were mandatory evacuation zones based on storm surge predictions. Our home is 27-feet above sea level, so we weren't anywhere close to being in any area at risk of a surge. However, we live a few blocks from the water, up a hill, so our house was technically within the colored area of the map for evacuations.

Madeline's mom was worried, so they evacuated to Orlando and took Madeline with them, which meant we didn't need to worry about her and her safety. She would be far away and safe with her mom.

With 3 cats and an old dog, no hotel would take us, and no over-crowded and unhealthy shelter seemed like a viable option. My parents' encouraged us to leave over the phone. Their encouragement quickly turned into begging and then yelling. I debated evacuating merely to keep the peace, but there was still the concern for our pets.

Tuesday, we prepped and watched the weather. It would be a Category 2, maybe 3. We discovered *AirBnB's* that were free for people evacuating and pet-friendly. That could work. We considered it, but quickly discovered they were all booked.

Then, suddenly, it was too late. At 12:30 a.m. Wednesday morning, October 10th, an alarm went off on my phone waking us. It indicated the storm could possibly reach Cat 4. It was going to hit by noon. We immediately implemented our back-up plan—go to *CityArts*.

Built as an armory with poured-concrete ceilings and more, it was the safest place we knew of. We packed food, water, and supplies into our van along with our dog, Charlie, and 3 cats— Coraline, Callaway, and Dazzy. Once we got everyone and everything inside the co-op, we pulled the futon mattress from the lounge into the dance studio to sleep. The lounge was open to the staircase to the 2nd level and we didn't want the cats to get into all the stuff in the studios. We slept on the dance studio floor, with Charlie at our feet, and three confused cats.

In the morning it started to feel like more hype, as all we saw were mild signs of an approaching storm. Honestly, it seemed to me that this time would be no different than all the ones before. I texted my mom every hour as requested to let her know we were fine. I checked the local news on my phone and began to become dismayed when all emergency responders and services were suspended. We were on our own.

By 11 a.m. we lost power and by noon wind speeds dramatically increased. We moved back into the lounge, an internal room without windows. I no longer had phone service. We blocked off the stairs with large metal grates, so the cats wouldn't get into trouble upstairs or be near windows. Large barn doors separated the lounge from the front gallery and the classroom that housed all the gallery's art. On Monday night we'd taken what, at the time, had seemed to be an unnecessary precaution, and removed the art from the gallery placing it in the interior of the classroom. The gallery faced two very large plate-glass windows and glass doors. We'd decided to play it safe.

As we corralled the cats and dog, every now and then we'd slide the barn door open a few inches to watch the wind and rain outside the large expanse of glass. Small objects traveling too fast or too obscured to recognize became larger and larger. It became difficult to see the house across the street at all. The constant force of the wind was unlike anything I'd ever seen. The long metal awning of *CityArts* began to bend, lift, and break. It soon became too risky to look outside, even from 30-or 40-feet away.

We sat on the couch in the lounge. We heard a loud clank of metal striking glass. We knew it must have been an awning rod striking the window. We shot each other a wide-eyed look as we heard it clank again and again. It was time to move into the bathroom—the safest spot in the building. As we gathered our most basic supplies and the cat carriers, we could hear the giant sheet of glass begin to splinter and crack. We sheltered in a small, interior bathroom. Three cats stacked in their carriers in the shower, while Mat, Charlie, and I sat on the floor.

Not long after, we heard an alarming crash and shattering of the glass barrier between us and the determined winds. Wind was now whipping inside the gallery. Mat started to leave the bathroom. I tried to stop him until I realized we needed to secure the barn door between the gallery and the lounge.

I followed Mat to see the barn door lifting against its hinges, threatening to fly free of the rail and allowing the winds to come further into the building. We managed to prop a heavy futon in front of the door preventing it from lifting. Mat then grabbed a gallery seating cube and wedged it in between the couch and the metal stairs to prevent the doors from forcing the couch forward. We retreated back into the bathroom, closed the door, and waited.

It was hot and dark with only the small flickering of a votive candle lighting our space. While the interior wood-based walls shook, we knew the armory-grade concrete was holding strong. We were scared, but able to joke about it to relieve the strain. What was sobering was the amount of panic and concern I knew my parents must be going through. With no means of communication, we couldn't let anyone know we were ok.

Through the muffled sound of harrowing winds, we theorized about the amount of damage and recovery time. More than days this time, it could be weeks and weeks, we thought. I was concerned about losing income from the 6-weeks of art classes already scheduled. Looking back now, we realized how much we didn't know.

How could we understand then, the severity and the extent of what was going on outside?

Hours passed. We couldn't believe the wind was still blowing so ferociously around us. Finally, the sound slowly dimmed. We couldn't stand the unknown any more. We emerged slowly.

Before we'd even left the lounge, a sudden loud bang halted us. The noise was followed by the same sound again and again at lower and then higher volumes. We peered out from the cracked, sliding door but couldn't see the cause. The slamming was inconsistent, and at times so loud it made us jump. Eventually, Mat ventured out of the lounge, crawling over the couch.

The wind had died with only sporadic gusts and almost melodic howls. The slamming we were hearing was the door between Mat's shop and the business next door. Mat secured it temporarily.

Thousands of tiny shards of glass, debris, and puddles of water littered the gallery floor and Mat's hand-made counter. His chalkboard menu had broken free of one of the wires and hung backwards, crooked, and swinging on the wall. The remnants of the vast window were now just jagged-edged remains lining the frame.

When I finally crawled over the couch, through the barn door, and walked across the gallery to look out the window, the sight that greeted me will forever be stamped in my memory.

Before the storm, I sat on that window sill often, talking to Mat while he prepared espresso. Gazing out into McKenzie Park, which housed numerous giant multi-hundred-year old oaks that created a dense green canopy of leaves and dancing, dangling Spanish moss.

As I looked out that same window now, my eyes widened, and the breath left my lungs. My heart sank. I didn't recognize what I was looking at. I couldn't believe my eyes. It was as if someone had picked me up and then set me down somewhere completely different.

Against the hurricane-grey sky, the tall, dark skeletons of the trees left standing were silhouetted. Their brothers laid out sideways with their roots exposed and the ground around them lifted and gaping. Giant branches were strewn across the landscape, snapped off, broken. There were no smaller branches in sight. Strips of metal hung from completely bare branches. It took a moment for me to realize why everything looked so alien. There were no leaves. Anywhere. None.

Harrison Avenue, the main thoroughfare in downtown Panama City, FL was in shambles after the storm. The Historic Martin Theater, which first opened in 1936, sustained costly damage. *Photo by Jack Hamm*

In Florida, most of the trees keep their leaves year-round. But that day the green left us. Spindly broken branches stood naked. All around them, more sky than we'd ever seen before. For the first time ever, we could see through the park to the buildings on the other side, now battered and damaged from the storm. The view was barren, devoid, empty, and stripped.

The following hours were filled with a frantic search for a phone with service while driving and walking through the remains of what was once Historic Downtown Panama City. Shattered windows, mangled roofs, trees and rubble blocking the roads. Standing water blocks away from St. Andrew's Bay. Business signs and awnings completely ripped off some of the still-standing buildings, and nowhere in sight. Other buildings were reduced to piles of bricks now littering the sidewalks and streets.

There were a few people out, moving slowly, also in shock. We spoke to everyone we saw and asked them if they were okay. They asked us the same.

We found someone with cell service, but it was weak, and I couldn't get a call through. I texted my mom that we were okay, but the sending status bar never reached its end before I had to hand the phone back.

We made it back to the co-op in disbelief. I stayed with Charlie and the cats while Mat went to check our house. I laid on the couch, still blocking the barn door, and cuddled with Charlie as I worried about Mat driving through fallen trees and power lines and reaching our home, only to find that it was gone.

Suddenly I realized how vulnerable I was—alone in a large building in an almost deserted downtown with no way of calling anyone for help. I found a hammer and kept it close.

Mat returned, and I was so relieved that he was okay that I momentarily forgot about our house. We sat on the couch, still blocking the barn door, as he showed me photos of what he'd seen.

When he pulled up the first photo of our street, I thought he must be mistaken. But he assured me this was our street. He showed me photos of our yard and our house. Only it wasn't our yard anymore, not as I remembered it. It was completely unrecognizable. No leaves, no trees, the ground covered with a huge mangle of bare, distorted branches.

Photos of our house were a surreal collection of images. Giant holes in the ceiling dumped out disgusting piles of wood and loose, wet, grimy insulation, which now covered our floors and furniture. Splatters of moist brown liquid covered the lower half of the walls. A thick branch shoved through the ceiling directly over Madeline's bed. The dining room, kitchen, hall, and Madeline's room were a mishmash of art, belongings, and furniture we were familiar with surrounded by gross piles of splattered, unfamiliar waste. And yet, our living room, guestroom, bathroom, and bedroom, were untouched—just as we'd left them. The stark contrast was unsettling.

Our laundry room was by far the worst, left in absolute shambles. A 3-foot tree trunk laid across the caved-in roof. Ceiling boards hung at waist-height, insulation balanced in between. My art studio, while difficult to get to through the numerous fallen trees, was untouched. Whole. I can still hear Mat saying both sadly and somewhat matter-of-factly, "And the focus is totaled."

Photos showed our little blue hatch-back car pinned under a pine tree that caved in the roof and windshield. I didn't even care.

As Mat described our house and yard, he began to cry, and I quickly joined. We held each other and let the tears stream down our faces.

A little while later, we heard a car pulling up and were hopeful it was Mat's parents. They lived about 45-minutes east of us in Wewahitchka, but much farther inland. The car however turned out to be Julie, our newest member at CityArts. She'd ridden out the storm in a public shelter, but felt it was too crowded, unsanitary, and miserable to stay in. She'd tried to drive to her house from every direction possible, but the roads were all blocked by fallen trees and poles. She couldn't reach her home. She seemed shaken, but immensely relieved and grateful to have somewhere safe to be with people she trusted.

And her phone had signal! I called my parents first and assured them we were okay. I cried as I told them I was so sorry we didn't leave and that we'd put them through so much worry. Mat called his parents. While many of their 12 trees were down, they and their home were okay.

I called Madeline to let her know we were okay. I had hoped she hadn't been watching the news and was somewhat blissfully unaware of how bad things were. I tried to keep it together and thought I had. Later, she'd tell me I'd been sobbing as we spoke.

While on the phone with her, I realized I didn't know what to say, how to protect her from this horror, or to begin to prepare her. I wanted her to know that she'd face a world quite different than the one she'd known. I told her she wouldn't recognize her hometown, but that we'd figure it out and it would be okay. I was telling myself that too.

As Mat and I laid down to try to sleep that night we held each other. I closed my eyes and eventually remained somewhere between sleep and dream for a long while, bizarre unrelated hallucinations dancing across my eyelids. Without any concept of what tomorrow would bring, any sense of time beyond the sun rising and setting seemed like an illusion.

Awake early the morning after the storm, we felt aimless. Luckily, with a dog, you know the first thing you have to do is take them outside. So, I leashed Charlie and walked outside, mentally preparing myself for what I'd see.

Every direction held endless damage and destruction—fallen trees, broken trunks, roofs ripped into ribbons or missing entirely, power lines mangled on the streets, twisted pieces of metal strewn about, nameless debris everywhere, and still no leaves in the awkward remains of what few trees were left. Every path Charlie and I walked wound around, under, and over giant obstacles. I had to carry Charlie often.

Despite the destruction, there were no sirens of any kind, only a few security alarms from businesses that rang constantly throughout the night. Every now and then a chopper flew above; News, National Guard, Coast Guard, and some unidentified. I wondered what they must be thinking of all this from way up there. Could they tell how bad it was? Or did it look worse from above?

Michael's winds were so strong that strips of metal from boat hangars were wrapped around the damaged hulls of boats in the vicinity of Watson Bayou and the City Marina in Downtown Panama City. *Photo by Terry Kelly/iStock*

I saw several people sitting on a porch by the Bayou Joe's Marina. A shy person, I normally would keep walking, but I waved, and they waved so I walked up to check on them. They asked how I was doing.

"Probably about the same as you," I replied.

"That's right, we're all the same now," one guy said.

Later that morning, after some random sweeping, checking in on people we saw walking by and giving them some of Mat's camp-stove coffee, we packed up and made our way to what remained of our home.

Making it to the front door was difficult as we stepped over and climbed under large fallen branches. The same branches I used to watch squirrels playing in were now scraping across my legs and arms. Seeing it in person, I cried. It was obvious we couldn't live there with giant openings in the ceiling, wet insulation everywhere, and questionable structural integrity.

We got word that people weren't being allowed back into Bay County. All information travelling by word of mouth, as no one had service or power. The whole neighborhood buzzed with various panicked efforts. Not knowing when or even if we would return, or if looting might be an issue, or if more rain would ruin our belongings, we packed.

We collected basic food, water, and other survival essentials. We packed a few changes of clothes and small items of sentimental meaning. We chose items we thought Madeline would want saved, too. We were limited on time since we had no idea the condition of the roads—traffic from evacuations, blocked roads from trees and power poles, and other unpredictability's. We decided to go to Mat's parents' house in Wewahitchka, even though we had no way of calling them. We hoped they hadn't abandoned their home, too. Normally a 45-minute drive we realized it could take hours and we wanted to arrive before sunset.

After hurried and scattered packing, we set out with our three very freaked-out cats and Charlie. Every block travelled presented new horrors. It was incredibly surreal. Our surroundings looked worse than any scene from every post-apocalyptic film I'd ever seen. Stores we had shopped in for years were stripped of their signage and store-fronts. Looking through shattered windows you could often see daylight shining through non-existent roofs. Roofs that now lay on top of chaotic tangles of pipes, shelves, and fallen products.

And there was just so much sky. Everywhere—so much glaring blue sky that used to be obscured by miles of trees. Once upon a time, past Panama City, Millville, and Callaway, the road to Wewa had been mostly tall, long-needle pine trees. But as the horizon continually rolled towards us, we saw endless acres of pines snapped in half like tooth-picks. Some areas included severely bent trees, almost as if they were frozen in that position when the wind forced them awkwardly toward the ground.

The Massalina Bayou Marina, where Bayou Joe's is located, suffered severe damage. In some areas, boats were stacked on top of each other, lying crippled where they'd been pushed by the strong winds and storm surge. *Photo by Jack Hamm*

We picked up a young man walking on the side of the road. He had no back pack—no bag at all; just a book and a couple other small items in one hand. He didn't really know where he was going or how far he'd have to walk. He just knew he needed to get away. His apartment had been destroyed. We offered him a ride and some water.

Just 24-hours after the storm dozens and dozens of fallen trees had been shoved out of the roadway or sawed in half to leave a cleared space just large enough for one car to fit through. Still, we drove over pavement littered with branches, debris, and tangles of power lines.

We passed empty cars in ditches, rushed by trees, or laying sideways. It felt like we were fleeing a war zone—unsafe, unpredictable, uninhabitable.

About halfway to Wewa there were more trees still standing. Entering the small town, we saw severe damage to trees and structures, but it was nothing like Panama City. It was recognizable. We felt like we knew where we were. There were more trees standing and they still had leaves on their branches. We dropped off the young man in the center of the small town, as he'd requested, and wished him the best.

As the sun lowered just over the horizon, we crossed West Arm Creek just before Mat's parents' street and we both began to weep. Tears of loss and of hope; tears of relief to be in a familiar place. Pulling into the driveway, I hugged Charlie tight.

Many trees were down in their yard, but through fallen branches we could see Betsy and Xelle sitting on the porch of their house, just as they often did when expecting us for a Saturday visit. We kept crying freely as they met us at our van.

"Well, is Panama City as bad as this?" they asked, clearly expecting us to say no.

Through a quivering voice and tear-streaked cheeks I said, "This looks GREAT. There're still trees, and they still have leaves! Panama City— it's a wasteland."

That night (and the following weeks) we had no power and no running water, but we had a hot meal—our first meal since before the storm. We'd only had a few handfuls of peanuts and raisins, hurried and busy as we were. Mostly, we hadn't eaten because we didn't have an appetite—we were in shock. But in Betsy and Xelle's familiar and cozy home, even dark and without power, it was warm and safe. We finally stuffed our bellies full.

Little did I know that the worst was not behind us. As I write this, now almost three months after the day that changed our lives, each day has been a struggle. Some days are a physical struggle, some days mental, some days emotional. But they've all been a struggle.

In the downtown area of Panama City, buildings that have stood since the early part of the 20th Century were reduced to piles of rubble. Much of the falling debris and wind-tossed tree limbs demolishing vehicles, boats, and neighboring businesses. *Photo by Jack Hamm*

We are still in the beginning. The first few weeks we were grateful for our lives and in survival mode—how to get food and water, how to bathe, how to cook. Once our basic needs were met we were faced with more difficult tasks and realities. If you didn't know any better, sometimes you'd look outside and swear the hurricane had just happened the day before. It's not for a lack of effort, it's just so much destruction. All our efforts seem like tiny dents in the grand scheme of it all. For so long it was such drastic chaos and the destruction felt surreal. We thought that was the worst it would be. But it wasn't. What's worse is when surreal turns into reality. It's this new reality we have to live in now, day after day, hour after hour.

◆ ◆ ◆

PROGRESS

The sound of hammering
The rapid staccato of nail guns
signalling neighbors
getting new roofs.
Shingles and metal
replacing blue tarps.
Up and down streets,
storage pods sit,
sheltering valuables saved,
as interiors are gutted,
and renewed.
Progress.

Businesses reopening,
a few at a time,
doing their best to serve
ravaged communities.
Some will never return.
Others will never be the same.

Children returning to school,
sharing classrooms
on useable campuses,
grateful for the portables
for their teachers
for the few hours of normal
each day brings.
Progress.

Debris piles growing smaller.
Twenty years of trash
collected in three months.
The rumble of trucks
bearing massive loads
a constant sound.

Trees that destroyed homes,
demolished power lines,

obliterated cables,
internet, cell coverage, HBO,
gone now.
Those still standing
showing signs of new growth.
Wisps of green decorating
stripped branches.
The skeletal look fading.
HBO and Google
returned to some.
Progress.

The Base has been open
for a month.
Units operational.
Though work remains.
Rebuilding Repairing.
Reshaping.
A base for the future.
Small victories.

A few miles away,
sagging stilt homes
keep vigil over discarded ruins,
indistinguishable remnants of life.
Salt water swamped palms
turned brown and yellow
slump over sand-covered
sidewalks bearing treads
marking the repeated passing
of bulldozers and dump trucks.
The smack of hammers,
hum of heavy machines,
camaraderie of out-of-town
contractors breaking for lunch,
invading the once tranquil
three-mile stretch of coast.
Where the eye passed.
Progress.
Slow and steady.

100,000 trees
planted by 2025.
The first, just last week.

A 30-foot,
15-year-old
cathedral live oak.
A symbol of what was lost.
A symbol of what can be.
A symbol of hope.
Progress.

—Jennifer N. Fenwick, *January 15, 2019*

As time passes, signs of new life are glimpsed throughout the Panhandle. Trees bearing new leaves. Piles of debris removed and streets returning to a cleaner version of what they have been since October 10. Fewer blue tarps gracing roofs as repairs continue. It's slow and steady but progress, nonetheless. #850strong #panhandlestrong

In the middle of the raging storm,
the wind grew still, the light took form.
All was calm for a single breath,
as I passed through the valley of death.

In the silence, my voice cried out,
take my fear, Lord, take my doubt.
Deliver me from this violent storm,
Protect my soul, Lord, bruised and torn.

Then, above the wind, I heard Your voice,
Clear and stronger than the noise.
"Come to Me, My beloved daughter,
Take My hand, walk on the water."

"I wait for you on the other side,
beyond the wind and the rising tide.
It's here, with faith, your eyes will see,
Peace will return, just trust in Me."

—Jennifer N. Fenwick, *January 24, 2019*

THE FACTS

Hurricane Michael, 2018

Hurricane Michael wreaked havoc along Florida's panhandle at CAT 4 intensity on October 10, 2018. At landfall, Michael brought with him sustained winds of 155-mph – 2 miles shy of a CAT 5 – and a minimum central pressure of 919 mb, the third-lowest ever to hit the continental U.S. Michael's barometric pressure was three millibars lower than Hurricane Andrew's (1992) lowest recorded pressure.

While post-storm analysis is still being performed and the argument surrounding upgrading Michael to CAT 5 is ongoing, the facts remain, this storm was a monster bringing widespread, apocalyptic destruction to the Florida Panhandle that will take years to heal.

LANDFALL: Michael made landfall at 12:15 p.m. local time on October 10, near Mexico Beach, FL

STRENGTH: High-end CAT 4 with sustained wind speeds at 250 KM/H or 155-MPH; Minimum central pressure, 919 MB. The Florida Panhandle took the brunt of Michael's fury, suffering apocalyptic damage as the storm peeled off rooftops, uprooted and snapped trees in half, destroyed homes and businesses, and caused extensive flooding.

HISTORICAL: Michael was the strongest storm to ever come ashore in the Florida Panhandle, as well as the first CAT 4 to make landfall in the area. Michael was the strongest storm to hit the U.S. since Hurricane Andrew in 1992 and Hurricane Camille, who in 1969, made landfall along the Mississippi Gulf Coast with 174-MPH peak winds and a storm surge of 24.6 FEET recorded in Pass Christian, MS.

STRONGEST WINDS OBSERVED: Tyndall Air Force Base, Florida recorded winds gusts reaching 224 KM/H or 139-MPH.

STORM SURGE: Apalachicola, FL recorded storm surge reaching 8.5 FEET. Near Mexico Beach, where the eye passed, National Weather Service buoy measured waves greater than 30-FEET before it stopped working.

OTHER FACTS: The death toll in Florida has risen to 35 in Florida and 45 overall, with at least 10 deaths reported in other states. Property damage following Michael is estimated at more than $4.5 billion. Damage to Florida's forestland is currently estimated at $3 billion.

There will never be another Hurricane Michael, as the name was retired following the 2018 Hurricane Season due to the storm's catastrophic intensity.

ABOUT THE AUTHOR

Jennifer N. Fenwick was born and raised in Panama City, FL. After marrying her husband, John, they moved to Phoenix, AZ where John was born, Three years later, they moved back to the Florida Panhandle to be closer to Jennifer's family and the members of John's family who now resided there. Their daughter, Nichole, now 29, was just one when they returned to Panama City. Their daughter, Emma, now 20, was born and raised in Panama City. Jennifer is a former Bay County teacher who now works professionally as a program analyst and technical editor for a government contractor. Her first book, *Four Weeks: A Journey from Darkness* was released on Amazon on October 6, just four days before Hurricane Michael hit the Gulf Coast.

In the Eye of the Storm: Stories of Survival and Hope from the Florida Panhandle is the result of the generous individuals who were willing to share their stories, their poetry, and their art with me. I am forever grateful for their generosity and the comfort and strength I found in sharing their words.

All royalties earned from the sale of this book are being donated to the United Way of Northwest Florida's Hurricane Michael Relief and Disaster Fund. 100% of all Hurricane Michael donations will be applied to LOCAL relief efforts in the Northwest Florida area. For donations visit http://unitedwaynwfl.org/

CPSIA information can be obtained
at www.ICGtesting.com
Printed in the USA
LVHW080850240319
611633LV00010B/97/P

9 781729 470480